To
Jonathan,

Romans 8:28

Laura and Bryan

Allen

BRAIN STORM

A Journey of Faith Through Brain Injury

LAURA AND BRUCE ALLEN

WestBow
PRESS
A DIVISION OF THOMAS NELSON

Scripture quotations are taken from the Holy Bible, New Living
Translation, copyright ©1996, 2004, 2007 by Tyndale House
Foundation. Used by permission of Tyndale House Publishers
Inc., Carol Stream, Illinois 60188. All rights reserved.

WestBow Press books may be ordered through booksellers or by contacting:

WestBow Press
A Division of Thomas Nelson
1663 Liberty Drive
Bloomington, IN 47403
www.westbowpress.com
1-(866) 928-1240

Because of the dynamic nature of the Internet, any web addresses or
links contained in this book may have changed since publication and
may no longer be valid. The views expressed in this work are solely those
of the author and do not necessarily reflect the views of the publisher,
and the publisher hereby disclaims any responsibility for them.

Any people depicted in stock imagery provided by Thinkstock are
models, and such images are being used for illustrative purposes only.

Certain stock imagery © Thinkstock.

ISBN: 978-1-4497-3772-6 (sc)
ISBN: 978-1-4497-3771-9 (hc)
ISBN: 978-1-4497-3773-3(e)

Library of Congress Control Number: 2012901209

Printed in the United States of America

WestBow Press rev. date: 02/01/2012

What Others Are Saying—

"*Brain Storm* is a true story of faith, family, community, and God's love—and the sheer will to recover. It is told in an extremely positive and uplifting manner. This book is a down-to-earth, practical, yet real presentation of the frightening, often gut-wrenching truths and experiences associated with a brain injury. The reader is clearly allowed to travel through the storm of a brain injury from the unique perspectives of both the survivor and the caregiver. *Brain Storm* is a *must read* for brain injury survivors and their caregiver, family, and friends—and for anyone needing to understand and believe that you *can* 'weather the storm' to become a better person than before."

—Ann Boriskie
Director of the Brain Injury Peer Visitor Association®, Georgia
(also a brain injury survivor)

"*Brain Storm* is not just the story of a man's experience recovering from brain injury, but it is also one of loss, grief, acceptance, and transcendence to find one's purpose in life. Bruce Allen's condition left him partially blind, without speech, and weak on his right side. His world was turned upside down. I was fortunate to witness the faith, hope, and hard work put in by both Bruce and his wife, Laura, as they regained their lives with grace and dignity. Bruce now gives back to others suffering similar fates with his frequent peer support and through this wonderful book. *Brain Storm* is a true testament to how fragile our lives are and how resilient we can be in the face of adversity. Bruce's story is an inspiration to me, his physician and friend, and will be to you as well."

—Darryl L. Kaelin, MD
Division Chief, Physical Medicine & Rehabilitation
Department of Neurological Surgery
University of Louisville
Louisville, Kentucky

"Bruce and Laura Allen have allowed us to journey with them in their remarkable, honest, painful, and miraculous story of faith, hope, and love. As their friend, I personally witnessed their 'Brain Storm.' This is a must read for anyone walking through extended physical suffering either as a patient, caregiver, or family member. You will laugh, cry, and rejoice—but most of all you will experience God."

—**Dr. Mark L. Walker**
Senior Pastor
Mount Paran North Church of God
Marietta, Georgia

"I discovered many years ago that life is tissue paper thin, and the trajectory of your life can change in a split second. My life-long friends, Bruce and Laura Allen, know this fact all too well, and they share their story of enduring a sudden storm that threatened to take Bruce's life in January of 2008. Their book, *Brain Storm*, will inspire every reader because of the way they encountered the adversity, and the ministry they developed out of the challenges they faced. I believe that trouble handled well always honors God. The Allens handled their situation with the maturity that only a deeply committed believer can possess in a time of great uncertainty, and they honored God with an unwavering faith. This is a book that people will need at some point in their life's journey either for themselves or someone they love. We all will encounter our storms, and the hope the Allens give us will help see us through!"

—**Dr. Dwight "Ike" Reighard**
CEO MUST Ministries
Lead Pastor
Piedmont Church
Marietta, Georgia

"Very early in the beyond belief and dangerously near-tragic challenges of Bruce and Laura Allen, I recall saying to them, 'Are you journaling your thoughts and feelings? You know this is a real, stuff-of-life story that ultimately will be a powerful witness of the keeping grace and miraculous power of our God, and a testimony of your resolve to trust Him.'

Brain Storm is indeed that story, now told by the two people who lived it—together! It is the story of a man of God, a preacher of the Word, now called upon to live out his faith and be patiently willing to take 'baby steps,' when his heart wanted to leap tall buildings in recovery. And importantly, it is the story of his faithful, resolute wife and companion, who processed each day of their journey with patience, fortitude, and great hope!

I commend *Brain Storm* to you, and my two special friends who lived it out—Bruce and Laura Allen!"

—Pastor James Byrd
Middle and Senior Adult Ministries
Mount Paran North Church of God
Marietta, Georgia

"Bruce and Laura Allen have a wealth of experience through pastoring, and are strong communicators. They have been tested by the fire of brain surgery and have confirmed that with God leading, when storms come your way, your fear doesn't increase, but your faith does. There is no doubt *Brain Storm* will challenge you, inspire you, and provide practical helps for people who encounter a 'brain storm.'"

—Rev. Jeffrey Hawkins
Pastor
Belmont Baptist Church
Calhoun, Georgia

"*Brain Storm* is the revelation of a couple's journey into the unexpected, with the grace of God to guide them through. It is the modern-day version of Second Corinthians 12:9, 'My grace is all you need. My power works best in weakness.' We can all learn from this captivating story."

—Dr. Charlie Howell
Pastor
First Baptist Church
Blue Ridge, Georgia

Dedication

Brain Storm is dedicated to brain injury
survivors who cannot tell their stories
and their caregivers who support,
encourage, and love them.

This book is also dedicated to all
rehabilitation therapists, doctors, and nurses
who continually inspire,
reassure, and help rebuild the lives of
brain injury survivors and their caregivers every day.

Contents

Forward

Many people write from their time of investigation, study, and learning; others have a story to tell through a personal experience. The Bible, even in its reference to salvation, speaks in the context of an experiential relationship and knowledge of Almighty God as opposed to intellectual curiosity. Bruce and Laura, in their new book, **Brain Storm: A Journey of Faith through Brain Injury,** speak to us about the trail as well as the trials that God took them through. I believe this book will serve as a source of encouragement to others who are survivors or care-givers of those who are going through a difficult time.

The Bible teaches in Second Corinthians 1:3 that we comfort others whereby we have been comforted by Almighty God. I believe that it is Bruce and Laura's sincere desire to use the contents of this book to be a source of encouragement that has the potential to fuel enthusiasm in the lives of those who are facing trials. It has been said that we are either in a storm, headed for one, or just coming out of one. Early in my ministry, I was challenged to always preach with encouragement, knowing that there were people on every pew with a broken heart. That is not just true in our churches, but also in our neighborhoods and the places where we work. People are in dire need of encouragement and someone to speak not just words of sympathy, but oftentimes empathy; not just concerned that you have been there, but sharing their journey of how they have been there and survived.

In Psalms 84:10, the Bible speaks of the Valley of Baca. We are told that this is not so much a geographical place but rather a spiritual reference—a place where we went through a dry season; but, before leaving, we dug a well and left an oasis for those who come behind us to be refreshed.

It is my prayer, and the prayer of the authors, that the words of this book will serve as a mighty source of encouragement for all who come through this place of difficulty. Read it, pass it along, and tell others. Everyone needs encouragement.

—Dr. Johnny Hunt
Senior Pastor
First Baptist Church
Woodstock, Georgia

Preface

Traveling this path of brain injury recovery, we did not find much available to read concerning what the patient is going through, how the caregivers can help and prepare themselves, or where to find resources and aids. Books with deep technological and medical terms can be found, but who needs all of that detailed information when you are in shock while dealing with a current brain injury in your family? We didn't want to build a brain. We wanted to know how to heal it. Much research had to be done to gather any helpful information. Who has time to scour the internet and dig in the library when you are spending every waking moment in the hospital or rehab center?

Brain Storm evolved as we maneuvered the maze of brain injury rehab and recovery. God led us to the right people and the right places at just the right time. After Bruce's formal rehab was finished, we discovered a group of brain injury survivors who meet monthly near our home. They have been a wonderful source of encouragement to us as we now travel this journey together. We learn so much from each other—survivor and caregiver alike.

We felt led to start a Saturday family support group that now meets weekly on the Brain Injury Unit at Shepherd Center. After two years of counseling with families who are in shock and are searching for help and encouragement, we saw a great need to put our thoughts in print. We decided to share what we have experienced in *Brain Storm* to hopefully be of support and encouragement to the thousands of patients who experience some form of brain injury each year and their caregivers.

Many people have contributed to this book by sharing their stories, editing these pages, and telling of the assistance they have found. Kelly Campbell, a brain injury survivor, spent countless hours reading and editing this book. Our good friend, Eric Howard, from Warner Robins, Georgia, also gave much of his time to proofread. Sue Cochran spent countless hours editing these pages to make this book the best it could possibly be. We owe a tremendous debt of gratitude to them for lending their efforts and excellent skills.

Ann Boriskie, director of the Brain Injury Peer Visitor Association, has been a close friend, confidant, and encourager as this project has come together. Ann trained us and made it possible to start the Saturday family support group at Shepherd Center. God had placed the dream for this group in our hearts when Bruce was a patient there, but it took over a year for it to become reality. Ann was the catalyst who opened the doors for this continuing ministry.

Including the stories of other brain injury survivors was a must. It was difficult to decide whose stories should be entered. Each person has a unique story of how he or she was initially affected and what he or she has gone through to achieve a "new normal." To give the perspective from survivors of a variety of brain injuries, nine people were asked and were happy to share their stories, with the hope that they will encourage others along the journey. They are wonderful examples to all of us of strength, determination, and perseverance.

Rachel, our daughter, has been a very special blessing. She happens to be (we love it when God's fingerprints are apparent all over a circumstance) a brain injury and spinal cord nurse at Shepherd Center. God placed her there three months before we took up residency. Her compassionate demeanor and loving approach has been evident during our stay in the hospital, going through outpatient rehab, and moving into the "real world." She was working the night shift after Bruce finished his formal rehab, so they shared lunch each day—which was *her* breakfast—and spent priceless time together. They would then run errands, which gave Bruce more real world therapy. Rachel is our special angel sent directly from God. She also did some proofreading for this project, which is not in her job description.

Of course, our families were a vital part of this entire journey. They have always been there for us, and they really went the extra mile to nurture and support us during this time.

A special thank you goes from our hearts to all who contributed and encouraged us in the creation of *Brain Storm*.

Introduction

The storm that entered our lives on January 7, 2008, took us totally by surprise. It did not, however, take God by surprise. When a life-changing experience comes our way, we have several options from which to choose. We can run to the internet, learn all we can, and try to make rational decisions—although we are in tremendous shock, and the decisions won't necessarily be rational. We can turn to friends, but they are often as clueless as we are, or we can turn to God and give Him complete control. We can praise Him in the massive storms that seem never-ending and impenetrable, and He can give us peace in our meltdown. He will actually take us to the other side—something we wouldn't want to do alone.

Storms constantly come our way. Winds of change blow through our lives. If we take refuge in God, we can trust Him completely. *Brain Storm* recounts how a storm of tremendous proportions came our way. More importantly, this is a story of how God sustained us and brought us through to an entirely new life—our new normal. When we trust Him completely, storms will touch us but not destroy us.

We want to share our journey of faith through brain injury to give hope and encouragement. Radical changes can happen—in the twinkling of an eye. Our story is about one of those unpredictable, unexpected moments. Our lives were altered dramatically in a matter of minutes. While writing this book, we have come to realize that even now, our story is still in progress. Rehabilitation is ongoing, and life is one big therapy lab.

This project was created with brain injury survivors and their caregivers in mind. It is our hope and prayer to give information, help, and hope in the following pages. We also are telling our story to bring awareness to the general public of what brain injury survivors may be experiencing, thinking, and feeling, and what can be done to help them.

I frequently wrote an updated email journal to our friends and family to keep them informed and help them pray more specifically. Most of the chapters in this book open with an actual email update. They haven't been doctored. As the caregiver, I follow by giving my reflections on what was going on at that moment, and then Bruce gives his thoughts from his unique perspective.

We'd like to tell you what we've experienced over the past four years as if you are sitting here with us. So relax. Have a cup of coffee and read as we share our recent journey with you. It may take some time, so I hope you have brewed a big pot!

Laura

Chapter 1

The Pain

LAURA'S THOUGHTS

UPDATE
Kennestone Hospital, Marietta, Georgia, January 3, 2008

After enduring three days of excruciating pain in his head for hours on end, Bruce had a CT scan today, and we learned that he has two tumors (probably malignant) on the left side of his brain, which affect his motor skills on his right side. We have an excellent neurosurgeon from Emory University Hospital who is going to do surgery next Thursday morning.

Love,
Laura

It was all such a whirlwind! New Year's Eve with the family at Papa's cabin included the normal fun and festivities. And then Bruce's headaches began. He had not been feeling well that day and asked me to drive to the cabin. Asking *me* to drive should have been a clue that something was wrong because usually he drove us everywhere.

Ibuprofen didn't help his dull headache. As midnight arrived, everyone celebrated, and Bruce went immediately to bed. By 5 a.m., he had progressed to horrendous head pain. The agony subsided somewhat, but we knew a trip to the doctor would be the first activity of 2008. As Bruce drove himself to the doctor that morning, I went on to work. Dr. Roaj Ujjin, our primary care physician, prescribed some medicine for the headaches and arranged for a CT scan. That's when things began to spiral out of control. Two days later, as he was getting ready to go for the CT scan, Bruce called me at my office saying something was terribly wrong. I rushed home and found my husband hardly able to walk.

By the time we arrived at the doctor's office, Bruce was disoriented and leaned heavily on me to get in the door. The receptionist could see that Bruce was definitely having difficulty walking and thinking, so she rushed us in for the CT scan. I told her we could not wait the normal couple of days for the results. Dr. Ujjin said for us to wait thirty minutes, and he would read the results immediately.

The downward spiral continued as Dr. Ujjin entered the examining room. His words were, "It's not good. You have two lesions in your brain, but I don't know what they are yet. Go immediately to the emergency room at Kennestone Hospital across the street, and a neurosurgeon will meet you there" (see Appendix A).

I couldn't deal with the reality that was presented to us. In shock, I was swept up in the whirlwind of the moments that swirled around us.

Bruce's Thoughts

On New Year's Eve, I started experiencing a headache. I'm not one to have headaches, but this one was very slight, so I thought nothing of it. After drinking some champagne at midnight, I felt worse. I blamed the headaches on the cheap champagne that my younger brother, Scott, had bought for this special occasion.

I went to bed right after midnight and immediately started having more severe headaches.

About 7 a.m., my seventy-five-year-old dad rose to grind beans for coffee—his favorite morning ritual. He was very surprised to find me already awake. I told him I couldn't sleep with this terrible pain in my head. I didn't feel right, so I ate a little breakfast with him. After Laura got up, I mentioned that we needed to go home. My dad responded, "Well, we have to clean this place up before you go." Cleaning the house was not on my agenda at the moment. I'm sure my dad thought that was an excuse—he loves to clean house, and I don't—but I reemphasized that I was in extreme pain and had to go home.

Because this was New Year's Day, no doctors' offices were open. Laura set an appointment with our primary care physician the first thing the next morning. When I saw the doctor, he prescribed some pain medicine and scheduled a CT scan for two days later. For most of that day as well as the next, I slept intermittently on the sofa. However, even with the pain pills and sleep, the agony was getting worse and continuing to build. My CT scan was the next day, so I thought I could bear it until then.

As I dressed to go to the doctor's office, I couldn't think clearly. I found myself sitting on the edge of the bed trying to figure out how to put my pants on and tighten the belt. I couldn't decide which leg to put in first or whether to put the pants over my head. It seemed like everything was very confused in my mind. In a moment of clarity, I called Laura at work. "I can't figure out how to get dressed. Can you come and take me to my doctor's appointment?"

She rushed home immediately. I couldn't get my arm up to put my shirt on, and then I couldn't button it. I knew things were not right, but I couldn't understand what was going on because it happened so gradually. As we got out of the car at the doctor's office, Laura had to hold me up since I was limping and very unsteady. By this time, I didn't know where I was going or why I was even there.

After my CT scan, Laura and I were taken to Dr. Ujjin's office to wait for the results. We knew by the expression on his face that the news was not good. When he told us I had two lesions in my brain, my mind went numb. What does this mean? Am I going to be okay? The possibilities sent me reeling incoherently, and I really couldn't un-jumble all my thoughts. I did what he told me to do, then stumbled from his office to the car to the hospital emergency room—and then waited—and waited.

I needed a suitcase of clothing for the hospital. I was not prepared. Laura reminded me that she could work all of that out later. Right now, the most important thing was to figure out what was going on in my brain. Whatever it was, we knew it was very serious.

Chapter 2

Tests and Preparation

LAURA'S THOUGHTS

UPDATE
Kennestone Hospital, January 4, 2008

Yesterday was a long day of tests for Bruce at the hospital, but Dr. Benedict let us spend the night at home. Then he called at 11 p.m. to say he had another idea and wanted to run more tests. We were there at 8 a.m. the next morning, did all the tests, and at 5 p.m. the doctor said he didn't discover what he had hoped. So we are back to dealing with the thought that Bruce has two malignant tumors.

Dr. Benedict has moved the surgery up to Monday afternoon. He doesn't want to wait until Thursday. Pray for us Sunday night as we meet with him at 6 p.m.—and also please pray throughout the surgery. Jason is flying in tonight, so we will all be together for this time in our family, and I am very grateful. This is happening so quickly. The doctor said three months ago Bruce probably didn't have this problem—this type of tumor grows rapidly—and it can come back.

We are still in shock, but we know that God is the Great Physician, and it is all in His hands.

D r. William Benedict, the neurosurgeon from Atlanta's Emory University Hospital, had recently been assigned to a newly established branch of the university called The Emory Clinic at Kennestone. A man of slight stature with a dry sense of humor, Dr. Benedict would talk with his patients like he had all the time in the world. God had been at work five months earlier in providing this newly established care center with the foremost neurosurgeon in the Southeast just three miles from our home. As our journey continued over the next year, we saw God's gentle hand repeatedly preparing the way.

Dr. Benedict sent us home with the plan to do surgery a week later. He ran some extra tests to see if the white blood cell count was elevated, which would indicate an infection instead of the malignant tumors that he suspected. The knowledge that our neurosurgeon was working on Bruce's case so intently at 11 p.m. brought me such peace.

The tests showed no infection, so we were back to square one preparing for malignant tumors—gliomas, the doctor called them. My vocabulary was really growing. However, the lesions were also rapidly growing, so the surgery was moved up to Monday. Bruce was immediately admitted to the hospital, and friends poured in for the next two days to offer prayer and support.

I knew I couldn't go into this life-changing event without the prayer support of our church family. So on Sunday morning, I typed up a brief paragraph and scurried over to our church, about a half mile from our home. As the congregation sang, I walked right up on the platform, handed the pastor my note, and sat down in the first pew. Our pastor knew Bruce well, and as he approached the pulpit, he said, "I've received a note that Bruce Allen is having brain surgery tomorrow for two malignant tumors. Let's pray right now for him." I felt so at peace and knew God was going to be right there with Dr. Benedict in the operating room.

Our son, Jason, flew in from San Francisco. It was very comforting to have him and our daughter, Rachel, by my side to offer encouragement and strong shoulders to lean on. On Sunday afternoon, Bruce's family, along with the four of us, met with Dr. Benedict. As the doctor who would be performing the surgery, Dr. Benedict wanted to discuss the details of the surgery.

As we sat around the conference table in the small hospital counseling room, Dr. Benedict held a replica of the brain in his hands. He meticulously explained where the problem was and step-by-step how the surgery would progress. There were two tumors, but he wouldn't know if they were malignant until he saw them. He planned to make an incision about eight inches long from above the left ear over the top of the skull. After folding back the scalp, he would remove a section of the skull and begin his work, depending on what he found. The surgery would take about three hours. With three preachers, a lawyer, a nurse, a pharmacist, and two medical professionals, the Allen family always has a multitude of questions. Dr. Benedict patiently answered every question we could think of.

When the information session was about to end, Bruce asked Dr. Benedict if we could pray together with him. There was such a sweet spirit as we all stood and held hands around the table. Bruce's father prayed for God to guide the surgeon's hands and give him wisdom the next day. We all felt God's presence in the room.

The evening was spent with more friends calling and coming by. A co-worker even provided a barbecue dinner with baked beans and corn on the cob from a local restaurant for everyone— about twenty people. It was actually a fun evening. We all were glad to have our minds distracted from the inevitable surgery the next day. Bruce was in good spirits and telling jokes!

BRUCE'S THOUGHTS

I don't remember going home from the emergency room that night. I had no idea that I would spend the next ten weeks in two hospitals and the following twenty weeks in rehab. I was just living in the moment—having tremendous headaches and wanting them to stop.

Once I was admitted to the hospital, medical personnel came into my room with increasing frequency—doctors wearing white coats, nurses in scrubs, and lots of other people. I could usually tell the difference between the doctor and a custodian pushing a mop bucket, but not always. One difference was the doctors had stethoscopes and seemed very interested in my breathing, my lungs, my pulse, and my blood pressure. They poked me, x-rayed my chest, ordered full body scans, and completed a multitude of other tests. I'm claustrophobic, so the MRI was definitely my least favorite After all, I was put in the machine head first. By the time I was taken out of that tube, fresh air never smelled so good.

My first day in the hospital actually wasn't too bad because I had a roommate—an older gentleman about ninety-two years old who was suffering from a lung infection. We had nice conversations and passed the night away.

The next day, many of my friends, fellow clergy, and church members came to the hospital to see me before the surgery. Of course, with the morphine, I felt like I was doing pretty well, even though the doctor had confirmed that the original brain scan was correct. Dr. Benedict had identified a fairly large mass in my left parietal lobe of the brain and a mass in my right occipital lobe. The friends and family who came by to show their love and encouragement before the surgery meant so very much to me as I faced the next day. Little did we know what awaited.

Chapter 3

Why Didn't We See the Signs?

LAURA'S THOUGHTS

As we waited for the actual surgery day to dawn, we gave much thought to the path to this moment. Were there any signs? Dr. Benedict asked what had happened to Bruce three weeks ago, because he could tell Bruce didn't have this problem at that time. Three weeks earlier, Bruce had had hemorrhoid surgery. It was an outpatient procedure, but when he arrived home, the antibiotic medicine made him sick to his stomach. When we called the doctor's office, the nurse said this reaction was common. She instructed Bruce to stop taking the antibiotic. We had hoped for a prescription for another medication, but she said to not worry. He didn't need to take an antibiotic. That didn't make sense for this type of surgery, but we did what she said.

The recovery from the hemorrhoid surgery was very painful, and Bruce was told recovery would take about three weeks. The doctor had prescribed Percocet for the pain. Bruce took it religiously to keep the agony at bay. One morning as he went outside to get the newspaper, Bruce's right leg gave way, but he caught himself before he fell. Bruce thought that was odd, but he didn't pay much attention to it even though it happened a few more times that week.

As a financial consultant for churches, Bruce's job required him to work on the computer a lot. He spent hours typing plans, projections, and emails—many, many emails. The day after his knee gave way, he sat down to type, but his is right hand would not respond. He thought maybe the Percocet made him sluggish, so he busied himself reading the paper. The words were a bit blurry—again, probably a reaction to the Percocet.

Our daughter, Rachel, had purchased her first home, and the second weekend of December was move-in day. We hired a group of men to move the big stuff. After the movers finished, our work began. However, when Bruce tried to help, he was clumsy trying to do anything. He couldn't hammer a nail (he really couldn't before this time, either), and he missed the table when placing a glass there. Frustrated, he decided to go home and get out of our way. Again, we blamed it on the Percocet. Later we realized we had placed the blame for his experiences on the pain medication instead of being aware that something much more serious was developing.

BRUCE'S THOUGHTS

During my post-op hemorrhoid surgery check-up, the doctor said it was completely normal to be in a great deal of pain for three weeks. However, a weakness developed on my right side. I was always a good speller, but now I struggled with spelling the smallest words. My thinking wasn't as clear as usual. I started having depth perception problems. The doctor had given me Percocet for the pain, so I thought it was making me dizzy and clumsy. These symptoms went on for three weeks, but I thought some rest would take care of things automatically. Boy, was I wrong.

All in all, I was feeling pretty good. I thought I would go back to work soon after Christmas. After all, that was why I had planned the operation during my Christmas break—so I could begin work again immediately after January 1. However, something didn't seem quite right after my doctor's visit. I talked to our daughter who is a nurse at Shepherd Catastrophic Hospital in Atlanta. She was concerned that these were the symptoms of a mini-stroke. I thought, "I'm too young to have a stroke—I'm only fifty-four!" My life was about to radically change forever.

Chapter 4

Surgery Day!

LAURA'S THOUGHTS

Surgery was planned for 2 p.m., but the nurses didn't take Bruce to the operating room until 6:30 p.m. The time passed *very* slowly. Since his surgery was moved up a few days, the surgeon had to squeeze him into the schedule. Unfortunately, the surgery ahead of him took longer than anticipated, which created a long afternoon of waiting. Jason's fiancée, Joanna in San Francisco, sent a lunch for all of us, and as we sat on the waiting room floor, we enjoyed our picnic. A few hours later, the nurse said it was finally time to go. After prayer, we made that long walk down the hall as Bruce was rolled to surgery. It all seemed so surreal. I apparently had watched too many TV hospital shows.

Sitting in the waiting room was numbing. We watched TV, read magazines and the paper, took phone calls, and tried to sleep. Rachel can't sit still for long, so she knew the long wait through the surgery would not be good for her. She decided to go on to her night shift work at the hospital, since the surgery was starting so late, in order to keep her mind off what was happening with her dad. We supported her decision. Jason and Bruce's family were there for comfort.

After only an hour and a half of surgery, Dr. Benedict appeared at the door and asked us to come into another smaller conference waiting room. Since the surgery was shorter than anticipated, we all were on pins and needles. We didn't know if that was a good or bad sign. "He didn't have any tumors. He had two abscesses!" We were so thrilled. I'm sure the folks in the waiting room wondered what all the shouting was about. I then asked the obvious. "What's an abscess?" He explained that an abscess was a pocket of infection. He was able to drain one, and now the antibiotic would remove any leftover infection. Hopefully, it would also kill the infection in the other abscess buried deep in the center of his brain. The surgeon said there would still be a lot of rehab and recovery time, but at least an abscess was treatable. Once again, we prayed with Dr. Benedict for the outcome of the surgery and for the days and months ahead.

Bruce was alert in the recovery area—and tired. We talked for a few moments, and I told him what had transpired. The nurse said it might be two or three hours before he was moved to neuro-ICU, and it was already 10:30 p.m. Bruce's family said they'd stay so that Jason and I could go on home. After calling Rachel at her work and rejoicing with her over the events of the night, I headed home for some much needed rest.

BRUCE'S THOUGHTS

On the actual day of my surgery, I don't think I was overly concerned about the surgery, even though I knew it was very serious. Many friends and family were there, and, of course, Laura was always there. I was laughing and having a good time. However, I did wonder if they would shave my head beforehand. Dr. Benedict said they would only shave the area where he would actually cut.

My family gathered around my bed that morning and prayed with me. We said our goodbyes with hugs and kisses. Laura said, "I'll see you later," which is what I always said when I left for work each morning. The nurses rolled me down the hallway out of the sight of my family. Being alone was a little scary—but then I realized I wasn't alone. God was right by my side.

The operating room was very cold, but one of the nurses put some warm blankets on me and told me I was going to be OK. A lot of people in scrubs, little hats, and masks scurried around the room. The lights shone brightly, and one of the doctors had his favorite music playing. Then someone asked if I was ready. I said, "Yes," and started counting backward from ten. I don't think I made it to nine. I honestly didn't worry about how serious this surgery could be. I thought it was something we could deal with, and then I'd go home and live my normal life as before. It's true: Ignorance *is* bliss. Pain and headaches are real. I knew I needed surgery, and I was ready for it immediately.

It is strange to be asleep on the table, not knowing where I am, and then wake up hearing someone say, "Mr. Allen? Mr. Allen, are you awake?" In fact, it's a little bit surreal. I was somewhat confused about where I had been, but I was thankful that I was not in a lot of pain and I didn't have any nausea. Everything seemed to be working. Laura said the surgery went fine, and I didn't have malignant tumors. My dad said, "Son, everything's going to be OK." All I had to do was lay there and recover.

Even though I was still under the effects of the anesthesia, I was becoming more and more awake. The nurses rolled me up to neuro-ICU, and I was starting to feel pretty good. I recognized my family and then dozed off for the night.

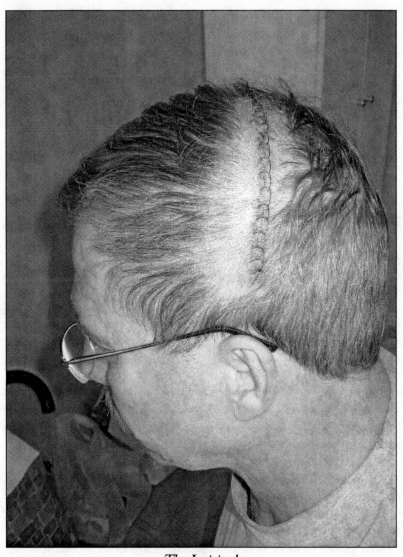

The Incision!

Chapter 5

Dealing with Reality

LAURA'S THOUGHTS

UPDATE
Kennestone Hospital, January 7, 2008, midnight

<u>Praise the Lord</u>! That is the most definitive thing I can say. They were abscesses—pockets of infection that the neurosurgeon was able to drain, and will now treat with high powered antibiotics. They are <u>not</u> malignant brain tumors as thought before. God <u>does</u> answer prayer—we knew that, but He proved it once again.

Dr. Benedict cut a three-inch by four-inch section out of Bruce's skull. The brain immediately began to swell, and he could see the main abscess (which was also three by four) very well. He drained it and decided to cover the skull hole with a plastic plate later after the swelling goes down.

Bruce and I both thank you for all of your prayers, visits, calls, and emails of encouragement. He will be in neuro-ICU for one or two days, in a regular room for one day, and then come home. He will take the heavy doses of antibiotics for about six weeks with constant CT scan and MRI monitoring, and then will be done with it all. The doctor said it will not return.

What a glorious day this has been.

Much Love,
Laura, Bruce, Jason, and Rachel

I didn't know how exhausted I was. Upon entering the house, I collapsed in my desk chair and typed out our wonderful update to send. When I stared at the wall as the thoughts of the day sank in, those tears that I had been avoiding for a week began to fall. The adrenaline I had been running on was gone. The whirlwind was subsiding just a bit, and reality was setting in.

Going through so many emotions, hearing so many new, shocking thoughts from the doctors, being surrounded by friends and family and yet feeling so alone can be overwhelming. Where would we go from here? I have to say, I never questioned my vow to be there "in sickness and in health." After all, that could have been me lying in that hospital bed as easily as it was Bruce, and the roles would be reversed. We had promised to care for one another no matter what, until we died. Walking out never entered my mind because of our commitment to one another and God.

I could try to face each day on my own and be a nervous wreck, or I could turn to God and ask Him to lead the way. Of course, I had been praying throughout the past few days, but praying when you don't know what you are dealing with is different than praying with the diagnosis in hand and knowing there is a long, uncharted road ahead.

I have an approach to seeking God's direction that Bruce has always made fun of. In total openness and seeking a true word from Him, I let the Bible fall open on my desk, and stab the page with my finger. Then I start reading. It really is amazing how God can speak directly to you this way when you are open to hear what He has to say.

When I was deciding if I should move as a young, single woman from New England to San Francisco (aka "The City") to go to Golden Gate Seminary, I did the "stab a verse" approach in desperation. Personally, I didn't want to leave New England, but I wanted to be sure God was leading in the next step of my journey. I had to know that I wasn't launching out into the unknown alone. As the Bible fell open, I stabbed Revelation 22:14—"Blessed are those who wash their robes. They will be permitted to enter through the **gates** of **the city** and eat the fruit from the tree of life." I certainly saw the part about entering the gates (Golden Gate Seminary) into the city (San Francisco)! I wanted to experience the fruit from the tree of life that was there for me, and I didn't see anything about the East Coast, Boston, snow, or New England. So, off I went. Living and ministering on the West Coast for four years was a wonderful experience—especially knowing that God was in the middle of it.

Years later, as a young married couple with a two-year-old, Bruce and I were given the opportunity to pastor a church in New England. He was born and raised in Atlanta, and living in New England—or anywhere else—had never crossed his mind. Of course, I had lived there as a single person and was ready for the adventure. When we couldn't find peace in the decision to either go or stay in Atlanta, Bruce, in exasperation, told me to stab a verse—which went against every grain in his body. We had been struggling with many concerns about moving to New England—distance from family, cultural differences, *snow*, and the fact that the kids would grow up talking funny. So I stabbed a verse—Acts 11:12. "The **Holy Spirit** told me **to go** with them and **not to worry**." In disbelief, Bruce asked, "What do you think that means?" I said, "I think the Holy Spirit is telling us to go and doubt nothing." So we were off to the northern winter wonderland and experienced four exciting, rewarding years of adventures with God there.

Now here I sat—seeking guidance, direction, solace, comfort, and a definite word from God. I knew I couldn't handle Bruce's brain surgery and recovery alone. The Bible fell open to Second Kings. I hadn't read in Second Kings in a long time, so it wasn't a familiar place for the pages to separate. I stabbed Second Kings 20:5. In this passage, Hezekiah is very ill, and the prophet

Isaiah informs him he is going to die. As Isaiah leaves, God tells him that he is wrong, and to go back to Hezekiah and proclaim, "I have heard your prayer and seen your tears. **I will heal you."**

Talk about a direct word from God! This definitely was one. You may not believe in the stabbing approach when seeking a strong word from God, but I certainly do. Such a peace came over me; the fear disappeared and the tears stopped. I promised God, "I'm taking your hand as a little child. I'm trusting you to guide us through this life experience every step of the way, because you have already shown me the outcome. So I'm going to hang on for dear life to your hand and believe your Word."

God doesn't always answer our prayers the way we'd like Him to. Too often we pray for Him to make things work out the way we want, but that is not always His perfect plan. The real purpose of prayer is to bring our lives into conformity with His will ("May your will be done," Matthew 6:10b), not to bring Him into conformity with what we want. Please read that sentence over again to let it soak in. Prayer is bringing our lives into conformity to His will. I have experienced a time when the death of a loved one was in God's plan, even though it was not my plan. However, I have found that His ways are perfect and mine are feeble at best. If circumstances always worked out the way I plan, we'd be in a mess. God sees the big picture and brings growth to us as well as to those around us. He will make our faith stronger through adversity if we will only take His hand and hold on for dear life.

The question "Why did this happen to Bruce?" has been asked often. Our question in reply has been, "Why not?" Just because we are Christians, we don't live a charmed life. The Bible tells us in Matthew 5:45 that God "gives his sunlight to both the evil and the good, and he sends rain on the just and the unjust alike." Believers and non-believers are all human and live on this earth together. We are faced with the same trials and obstacles day in and day out. The difference is how we, as believers, handle these difficulties. Bruce and I choose to trust God to walk us through. He never promised to take us out of the storm; rather, He will give us peace in the storm. Then God can and will bring good from the bad that comes our way. We'll talk about the good that has come from this situation in a later chapter.

However, for now, the night of my husband's brain surgery, I leaned heavily on the words from Second Kings 20:5—God will heal Bruce. I was holding on to His hand with a tight grip.

Chapter 6

Neuro-ICU, Our New Home

Laura's Thoughts

UPDATE
Kennestone Hospital, January 9, 2008

It is now two mornings after brain surgery—Bruce is somewhat groggy, tired, and has a large hole in his head, but other than that, everything is fine. Right now, it is just "wait and see." He's in neuro-ICU, and the doctors say he is responding extremely well. The nurse walked him briefly the morning after surgery—she also made him put on his socks and buckle a belt. The surgeon said the swelling is going down well. He also said that Bruce has a very serious infection, so we are waiting for the pathology report in two more days to see exactly what it is, where it came from, and what antibiotics to use against it. The surgeon is giving Bruce strong doses of general antibiotics until he knows in which direction to go. They won't put a plate in his head for six month—to cover the hole in his skull. I guess that cuts out sky diving for a while!

Keep praying. We're not out of the woods yet, but we can see the clearing in the distance. What a blessing for it to be these abscesses instead of malignant brain tumors as previously thought. God is so good.

Ah, life in the neuro-ICU. What an experience. Monitors beep everywhere, tubes weave all around the bed, meals don't arrive at any specific time, and the nurses are wonderful and compassionate—mostly. As we settled into our new home on the third floor neuro-ICU, we found it had everything we needed—a bed for Bruce as well a convertible bed and potty for me. This would be our home for the next five weeks. Originally, the doctor said we'd be out in five days, but God had other plans.

Dr. Benedict was wonderful. He came by the room two to three times a day and sat down to answer my volumes of questions. He treated Bruce as if he were his only patient. He said, "In a year, this will seem like a dream." Bruce responded, "More like a nightmare!" We had a long road ahead of us now that the surgery was actually over. As the reports came in, we learned it was a strep infection called streptococcus viridans that had probably originated in an incision for the hemorrhoid surgery. The infection traveled through the blood stream and settled in the brain. Two abscesses started to grow rapidly. Since the surgery, Bruce had been receiving some strong, general antibiotics, but now that Dr. Benedict knew the type of infection, he would begin eight weeks of IVs of Rocephin, a very strong antibiotic that would destroy any residual infection and hopefully decrease and destroy the second abscess. If the second abscess didn't decrease, he would have to drill a burr hole in the center of Bruce's skull in order to go in and drain it.

Bruce still had much weakness on his right side, but we were told that it would improve when the swelling subsided in his brain. His arm and leg were limp and had no feeling. After another MRI, we were made aware that the second abscess was not responding to the Rocephin. It had not shrunk, but it had not grown either. A second surgery to drain the abscess was necessary —quickly. The good news was that the original abscess was responding very well to the antibiotics, so Dr. Benedict anticipated the same results with the second abscess after it was drained.

The CT scan was done the next morning, and surgery was scheduled for 2 p.m. The doctor would drill a hole, go in with a needle to drain the abscess, and then put a catheter in the hole to continue the draining process after surgery. He asked if Bruce wanted to be awake or asleep during the surgery. Bruce replied, "Uh, I don't think I want to listen to the grinding of bone—especially when it is my skull." So he was knocked out for the two-hour surgery. Bruce was assured that he would see improvement in the way he felt after this procedure. Dr. Benedict said he would go into an area of Bruce's brain that isn't really used (boy, could I run with the jokes on that one!), so it shouldn't affect his thinking or motor nerves.

The nurses came to get Bruce for his 2 p.m. surgery at 8:40 p.m. When he returned to the room at 11 p.m., we received a good report. We needed to wait for the swelling to go down on both sides of his brain in order to see how much rehab he would need. Of course, he would be on the strong antibiotic for six to eight weeks while doing rehab. Dr. Benedict said it could be six months before Bruce would be back to full force. He could work from home on the phone after six weeks or so. This was a wonderful prognosis compared to the initial one of a malignant tumor.

BRUCE'S THOUGHTS

The morning after the first surgery, I remember eating some breakfast. I was able to use my arms, hands, and eyes just fine. I had no problems getting up to go to the bathroom, walking around the room a little bit, and going back to bed. Of course, I was aware of the bandage on my head where the craniotomy had been done, but I didn't really feel any pain. All I can say is, "Thank God for morphine."

Things were going pretty well in ICU, and I was sleeping as well as anybody can sleep there. The hospital helicopter pad was right outside my window, which flew night and day. I could hear the helicopters coming and going, but it really wasn't bothersome—it was kind of entertaining. I didn't need to wear the football helmet that sat so gracefully on the heads of many of my new craniotomy friends. I really don't know why, but I was glad.

The second surgery was a delicate one—probing into the center of my brain where my occipital lobe intercepts some very important parts of the brain. Of course, I've since learned there are no unimportant parts of the brain. Every piece of the brain has some particular function, whether seeing or regulating body temperature, pain sensors, feeling sensors, etc.

The surgery was brief. I had a new bandage around my head, and even though I hadn't shaved, bathed or shampooed in a week, I thought I looked pretty good. Dr. Benedict said everything went as expected in surgery. He moved me to a regular room out of the ICU the next day. In two days, if all went well, I could go home. That sounded great to me. I missed our home. I missed my dog. I missed the colors in our home. I wanted to sit in my swivel chair and rock and watch my widescreen TV. I wanted to look out in the backyard and watch the birds. I just wanted to go home.

Be still in the presence of the LORD,
and wait patiently for him to act.
Psalm 37:7

Chapter 7

The Night from Hell

LAURA'S THOUGHTS

UPDATE
Kennestone Hospital, January 15, 2008

Bruce may be able to come home Friday! Looking at him tonight after surgery makes that hard to believe, but I trust what his doctor says. I'll send you the (hopefully) last update when he comes home.

Now I know why doctors are said to practice medicine. It is definitely *not* an exact science, and practicing is about all they can do. The day following the second surgery was rough for Bruce. The drain catheter was removed from the burr hole. However, the swelling from surgery affected his vision, which we hoped would clear up as the swelling went down. The abscess was next to his occipital lobe, where the sight is controlled in the brain. His right side was still very much affected, and his mind and body were worn out after fourteen days in the hospital and two brain surgeries. He really needed physical and emotional strength for the days that lay ahead.

When the wires and tubes were disconnected, Bruce was moved from neuro-ICU to a regular floor. The move in the wheelchair really made the room spin for him. I asked the doctor how long it would take for the swelling to go down. He said, "It will take as long as it takes. Everyone is different." He was a wise man.

If the day of the second surgery was hard on Bruce, the night was worse. After the dizzying wheelchair ride down the elevator to the regular floor, he didn't know his name or where he was. It was an extremely frustrating twelve hours. I kept telling the nurses as each shift changed that something was terribly wrong. He was losing his speech, he couldn't see—and he needed to urinate but there was no urinal in the room! In times like this, the caregiver is a loved one's only advocate. I had to be persistent until I was able to get some help. The urinal appeared forty-five minutes later.

I continually asked the nurses to call Dr. Benedict. They said they would do it in a minute—but even after I had pleaded through three shifts of nurses, none of them called. Finally, when his office opened at 9 a.m., I called and told his receptionist of the situation. Dr. Benedict was in our room within fifteen minutes. He said he had been on call all night but never received one call about Bruce. He and I were both livid, so I won't go any further. Caregivers, be vigilant when you know something is wrong.

Bruce was immediately moved back to neuro-ICU, and another CT scan was done. The left frontal lobe of the brain was now rapidly swelling. Although this area was not involved in the previous surgeries, the left frontal lobe, where the speech area is located, was now affected. The doctor started two high-powered diuretics and anti-inflammatories to try to bring the swelling down. He didn't know if another abscess was trying to start or exactly what was causing the swelling. He stated that the brain is very erratic and does strange things like this. If the swelling continued, he would put Bruce on a ventilator to keep oxygen going to the brain and the body. If worse came to worse, Dr. Benedict would do surgery to relieve the swelling, but he really didn't want to do that unless it was the last resort. He said the brain had had enough intrusion. His last comment was, "He is very, very sick man."

I reminded God He had said He would heal Bruce, but things weren't looking that way at the moment. He then reminded me that I was losing my grip on His hand, and I'd better grab on again—with both hands! He also reminded me of my chosen life verse: "Trust in the Lord with all your heart; do not depend on your own understanding. Seek His will in all you do, and He will show you which path to take" Proverbs 3:5–6). I had to stop leaning on my own understanding—and hang on to His strong hand.

BRUCE'S THOUGHTS

Have I mentioned yet that life can turn on a dime? Well, it can. I was feeling good one day and having brain surgery the next. The night I was moved to the regular floor in the hospital proved to be one of those nights where everything changes. As I was taken from ICU in a wheelchair, the halls began to spin. I thought it was because I hadn't been up much during the past ten days. However, my brain had begun to swell for some reason, and everything was going to pot. Within an hour, I didn't know who Laura was, and I really didn't know where I was. I was slurring my words, I didn't know what I was saying, and I couldn't really think. I was terribly confused and disoriented. Then I noticed I couldn't see well. My vision was *very* limited. I could make out images, but not clearly. Everything seemed to move faster around me. Suddenly, nurses scurried in, people pushed carts, and moved my IV poles. Before I realized what was going on, I was back in neuro-ICU. I had lost my eyesight, speech, thinking ability, and complete use of my right side. It was worse than a stroke. All of a sudden, I knew what an acquired brain injury was all about. Would any of my abilities every come back?

And this same God who takes care of
me will supply all your needs.
Philippians 4:19

27

Chapter 8

In the Pit

Laura's Thoughts

UPDATE
Kennestone Hospital, January 17, 2008

Things improved ever so slightly this evening. The new swelling has stopped. Now we need to pray that the brain goes down to relieve the pressure and restore his speaking ability. He tries to say things, but the words just won't form, which frustrates and distresses him greatly. This afternoon he couldn't say anything. Tonight he said one or two short sentences. They were very hard to say, but he said them. I told him this was like a bad episode of the TV medical show, "House." He turned his head toward me, and very slowly said, "R-e-a-l-l-y!"

The newly swollen part of the brain affects his swallowing abilities as well. Unless the swelling goes down enough to allow him to swallow, the doctors will insert a feeding tube through his nose tomorrow. We'll have to wait and see how the swelling responds. I told him he was going to have a great story to tell when this is all over. He said, "Yeah."

Please pray for the swelling to go down, his speech to be restored, and his spirit to be lifted up on eagles' wings. Thank you again for being my prayer partners and supporters in this spiritual journey. I am receiving your emails of encouragement. Please forgive me for not answering them personally at this time. I know you understand.

When we moved back to the ICU floor the next morning, Bruce didn't know who I was, or couldn't express it verbally. Each following day was different in neuro-ICU, and gradually we saw slight glimmers of improvement. A few days later he was getting out four-word sentences, although it was very frustrating to him when he couldn't find the right words. He gradually knew who everyone was, was alert, and understood what doctors and nurses were telling him.

The next four weeks were crazy. Bruce lay in the bed. He couldn't sit up, see, or speak much, but he didn't seem to care. He had the easy part—just lay there. I had the tough part—stand by his side, try to keep him comfortable, and maintain a full-time job. My supervisor at work, Dr. Christina Horne, was more than gracious. My special coworkers even took up a collection of four hundred dollars to help with expenses. I went to work from 8 a.m. to 2 p.m. Dr. Horne, being the sensitive person that she was, then encouraged me to work from a computer at his hospital bedside from 3 p.m. to 6 p.m. I spent 6 p.m. to 9:30 p.m. with Bruce, and then went home to sleep until 6 a.m., when I would start all over. This schedule kept up for basically thirty-six weeks, including the hospital stays and the twenty weeks of rehab. Some friends have asked how I did it. My reply is, "You do what you have to do." However, caregivers really must take care of themselves and get lots of rest to be physically able to do what is required of them. If you think this in-patient time is draining, wait until your loved one comes home. Then you are *really* going to need to take care of yourself. Rest now while others are there to be the nurses.

Our families were so supportive. They visited regularly on the weekends, and relieved me some during the week so I could do laundry and other chores. Bruce's stepmother, Faye, fed him his meals since she had a lot of experience feeding her dad in the nursing home. Bruce said feeding someone is an art, and Faye was an expert. Melinda, his compassionate sister who is a pharmacist, stayed with him for entire days to give me a break. Scott and Brandi, Bruce's brother and wife, always visited with yummy cookies that frequently kept the nurses in our room. His father, John, came often to talk, read aloud to him, and be with his son, as did John and Angie, Faye's son and wife. With all of them and their children, along with the friends and our cousins who came by to bring music CDs, goodies, and laughter, we both were encouraged and energized.

Many hours were spent playing charades. Bruce would say, "I want..." and then I would try to guess the rest of the sentence. We had taken a personality test when we were married in which we only had two answers that were different out of five hundred questions. The psychologist said we were more alike than any two people he had interviewed. It could be boring because we always knew what the other one was thinking—or it could be helpful, because we would always know what the other was thinking. In playing "guess what I want" with Bruce, I could figure out what he wanted 80% of the time—getting a drink of water, giving a cookie, or scratching his nose.

I was giving Bruce a hand massage on the left hand—his good side—when he asked me to do the right hand. As I began rubbing, he said he could feel something! After three weeks of rubbing his arm, hand, and fingers with no feeling, he was finally getting a response. He could also feel my touch to his right cheek. Then we started "watching" TV, and he said he could see the people on the screen. During the Super Bowl, he had only seen a blur. He moved his right leg after three weeks of immobility. Apparently the swelling *was* finally going down.

After an extremely long day at my work, I arrived at the hospital at 3:30 p.m., instead of 2 p.m. I walked into the room and said, "Hi, Bruce." He angrily yelled, "Where have you been?" I was so shocked that he uttered—or yelled—a full sentence with more than two words that I could only answer, "My, our speech has certainly improved, hasn't it?" It continued to gradually improve each day—but I made sure I wasn't late again! That was the beginning of the return of his speech. There are times now when I miss those more quiet days—I'm just kidding. Many more months passed before his normal speech pattern returned, and even now, some words continue to elude him.

We have a dog named Princess who is part Jack Russell Terrier and part Shih Tzu. She's so ugly that she's cute. Princess was a freebie we found in the newspaper, and she is Bruce's lap dog. When Bruce is home, they are inseparable. I pinned an 8x10 picture of her on his bulletin board, even though he couldn't see. I knew someday he would. He really missed Princess, so a nurse suggested I bring her up to visit after four weeks in the hospital. I knew dogs were not allowed in the ICU, but I was encouraged to bring her up at 6:30 p.m., when the nurse shifts were changing, and stay only fifteen minutes. Bruce got as excited as he could, knowing she was coming. He wouldn't be able to see her, but he could feel her with his left, functioning hand.

I wrapped her in a baby blanket and entered the hospital through the rear entrance. No one was waiting to get on the elevator, so I jumped on with my bundle of joy. Two older ladies who had ridden up from the basement were already on the elevator. As we began to move, Princess wiggled in my arms. And then she wiggled more—and more. Finally, one of the ladies said, "My, you certainly have an active baby there." I pulled back the blanket and said, "Yes, and she's hairy, too!" We all had a good laugh together as I exited on the third floor. I scurried down the hall, ducked into our room, and closed the door and curtain. I put Princess on the bed. She was so excited to see Bruce, but she could tell something was really wrong. She lay down next to him and didn't move as he slowly reached out to pet her. It was a very bright and tender moment in a very dark and scary situation.

BRUCE'S THOUGHTS

While I was in neuro-ICU, one of the nurses, Bill, became a good friend. He talked to me about God. One day he brought a CD with soothing music and sat down on his break to listen with me. It was a great way to pass the time.

Laura smuggled Princess in one night when I was experiencing some depression. Having my little Princess in my arms was wonderful. She licked my face and was so happy to see me that she really did not notice all of the wires and bandages on my head. She brought a lot of joy to me during those moments. It's amazing what a little dog can do for a person with a brain injury. Without saying a word, she had changed my whole day from being somewhat gloomy into having a bright ray of sunshine.

Before the burr hole operation, I thought I would be going home in a few days. However, my condition certainly changed. Two days after that second surgery, I didn't know where I was. Clocks looked like strange, oblong shapes. My eyes, which had been crossed for three days, were not focusing or translating to the brain what they saw. I couldn't really visualize what was on the television without squinting, and even then, I could only see a small portion of the screen. The numbers on the clock were crazy-looking, but it didn't matter because I didn't know what a number was. Two plus two meant nothing. I had also lost my executive functions for planning and organizing. Voice recognition was my greatest asset. Gratefully, I never had long-term or short-term memory loss as many brain injury survivors do.

On Super Bowl Sunday, our neighbors, Charlotte and Charles Godfrey, with their daughter, Miranda, brought a shopping bag full of goodies decorated with love. That's the best kind of gift. As game time approached, I wanted to listen to the TV, but I couldn't communicate my desire to Laura. I motioned with my one good arm toward the big box on the wall. I was trying to think of the word "television" or "football," but neither one would surface. I had some memory issues and definitely had impaired cognitive thinking at this point, so I kept motioning toward the TV. The Super Bowl was a big game between the Patriots with Tom Brady and the New York Giants with Peyton Manning's little brother, Eli. However, I couldn't persuade her to turn on the TV. Finally, in my exasperation, I blurted out, "Tom Brady!" The nurse standing nearby said, "He wants to turn on the Super Bowl." That night I was able to listen to the game—not watch, but listen—and I felt complete as a man!

My brain was working, but it wasn't working right. I still felt pretty good, though, and I loved the morphine shots. They kept me going every six hours, and I could push the pain pump as often as I wanted. I couldn't tell whether anything was actually going in, but it was OK with me to feel good and not have any pain. Between the dog's visit, the morphine, and the good care that I received at Kennestone, I was very happy. Things were really looking up—or so I thought.

"For I know the plans I have for you," says the Lord.
"They are plans for good and not for disaster,
to give you a future and a hope."
Jeremiah 29:11

Chapter 9

The Next Step?

LAURA'S THOUGHTS

UPDATE
Kennestone Hospital, January 21, 2008

Dr. Benedict told us today that when Bruce moves out of the ICU (whenever that may be), he will go to inpatient rehab. I asked if there were any chance he could go to Shepherd Center in Atlanta, and he said he thought so. That would be wonderful! First, God gives us an Emory neurosurgeon at Kennestone Hospital, and then He may open the door for Bruce to go to Shepherd for rehab—which is one of the foremost facilities in the nation for spinal and brain injury rehab. (Of course, I'm not biased just because our daughter is a registered nurse there. However, that is why she went there—because it is the best.)

The physical and occupational therapists came by today. They said he is experiencing ataxia, which means the brain has forgotten what it is supposed to do. Bruce is going to have to learn to walk, feed himself, sit up on his own—which means reteaching the brain how to do all those things we take for granted. When the therapist said yesterday after her session, "He'll be able to walk again," a lump caught in my throat. That was never a question in my mind. It was good to hear an expert confirm what God has already promised! She was able to tell from how he responded to her session that he will be able to teach the brain what to do again through therapy at Shepherd Center!

Then Dr. Benedict told us tonight that in two weeks, he will be moving Bruce to Shepherd Center for rehabilitation. He needs acute physical and occupational therapy, and Shepherd Center is the best for both. Again, God is so good.

Bruce was improving s-l-o-w-l-y, but improving. His speech was much better—which meant he had gone back to not listening to me—and talking all the time. He still would get his words twisted a little. Rachel's clothes dryer's heating element went out. Bruce said, "Well, we need to replace her elephant." We all had a good laugh out of that—including Bruce.

Following five weeks in neuro-ICU, we started exploring where to go for rehab—either to Kennestone Hospital, Emory University Hospital, or Shepherd Center. The list of possibilities was endless and mind boggling. This decision had to be made soon because he was ready to begin rehab. Bruce had been lying in the bed for five weeks, and it was time to start moving. A physical therapist came in with an assistant to see if he could sit up. As she moved Bruce's legs to the side of the bed and raised his body up, he slumped like a rag doll to the left and then to the right. It appeared that he did not have a backbone at all. As I stood behind him, I was glad he couldn't see the shock on my face. He *had* to be able to sit up again. That had never crossed my mind either. I was ready for rehab to begin.

Arrangements began to be made to go to Shepherd Center. The case manager came to assess his situation. She said, "I'm amazed at his talking ability. He is so much better than the report we received five days ago." She planned to move him to Shepherd Center whenever a bed became available. Bruce was so ready to start rehab. He knew it was going to be hard work, but he was ready for it. He said, "I'm looking forward to getting my sight back." That was coming, too.

Bruce experienced a lot of abdominal pain during his last two weeks in ICU. He had no normal bowel or bladder movement because his right side was not functioning. He was bloated like a woman who was nine months pregnant. Instead of dealing with the cause of the bloating, he was given morphine and Percocet to mask the pain. We were told that the doctors at Shepherd Center would know how to deal with it. That definitely didn't solve the problem now, but it certainly made me look forward to the next step.

As Manley Beasley, the evangelist, often said, "Faith is believing something is so, when it is not so, in order for it to be so." God has proven that statement in our lives many times in the past, and we trusted Him to do it again. Bruce, Rachel, and I talked about how amazing it was that everything seemed to have been worked out in advance by God for this exact moment: Rachel started working as a nurse at Shepherd Center and educated us about it. A friend of ours was a patient there a year before, so we had seen first-hand the miracles brought about by rehab at Shepherd Center. Dr. Benedict opened the Emory Neurosurgical ICU at Kennestone Hospital last August—just for us. At our one-year checkup with Dr. Benedict, we thanked him profusely and said we knew that we had the best surgeon available. He replied, "You didn't have a choice. I was the one on call in the ER when you arrived!" We all knew that God *had* provided the best surgeon possible, and had scheduled him to be on call that day. Our two kids graduated and were settled in jobs and homes of their own, before this event entered our lives. We were free to focus on this part of the journey. There were too many "coincidences" for it all to be coincidental. God was so faithful—when we couldn't see in the darkness, He was and is still there.

BRUCE'S THOUGHTS

Each time the morphine shots began to wear off, I was in a great deal of pain. It seemed that my right side, especially my right leg, was on fire. I didn't know it at the time, but the pain in my leg was apparently nerve pain from messing with the brain. Everything in the body is directed by the brain. Sight, speech, feeling on the right side—everything. By lying there and taking a morphine shot every six hours, I was becoming a vegetable. I remember one morning, as two of my nurses came into my room, they looked like little Tinkerbells coming in with my breakfast and singing. I was very confused and disoriented. I was not getting any better; rather, I was continuing to lose function.

Getting up to go to the bathroom wasn't an issue any more. With the catheter in, I didn't have to get up, which seemed fine to me. However, another problem was developing. I hadn't had a bowel movement in about four or five weeks. The doctors gave me some medicine, but nothing worked.

It was becoming more evident that I needed to go somewhere else that specialized in brain injuries and rehabilitation. I was so out of it that I didn't really know what I needed. I'm so thankful that I had a good wife who was a wonderful caregiver and was constantly asking and seeking out what should happen next.

Despite all these things, overwhelming victory is ours
through Christ, who loved us.
Romans 8:37

Chapter 10

Shepherd Center Arrival

LAURA'S THOUGHTS

UPDATE
Shepherd Center, Atlanta, Georgia, February 9, 2008

Now the work begins. Bruce was transferred by ambulance to Shepherd Center on Wednesday and settled in. On Thursday, he received his own fitted wheelchair and took a shower for the first time in five weeks—he had had dish baths, but that is nothing like a full-fledged shower where you can wash your hair. Of course, the aides helped him as he sat in a chair especially made for the shower. He loved it! When he asked for his hair to be cut, the aide said, "I only do military cuts." Bruce said, "Go for it." Now he looks like Bruce Willis, but he says it feels so much better.

Shepherd Center is a wonderful place. It has all the equipment and expertise to do what Bruce needs done. They are also very nice people. Thursday night Bruce was having horrible pains in his head. The doctor said it was just the brain sending out mixed up messages. Pain medication was not helping. About midnight one of the aides came in and prayed with Bruce, and the pain subsided. He was able to sleep the rest of the night. This kind of sensitive person is who I want taking care of Bruce in times like this!

Bruce shed the hospital gowns and now wears pajamas, running suits, T-shirts, and Velcro tennis shoes. His spirits continue to be good. He knows it just takes time for the swelling to go down and the rehab to work, but determination is his strong characteristic right now.

Shepherd Center is a catastrophic hospital in Atlanta, Georgia, that focuses on spinal cord injuries, acquired brain injuries, traumatic brain injuries, and MS. It is one of the top ten rehabilitation hospitals in the nation; people come to Shepherd Center from all over the world. There was never a question of where we would want to go. After the Shepherd case manager assessed Bruce's situation and approved him for admittance, we were so excited at the prospects of what they could do to help him.

Finally, we were on our way to transitioning from surgery care to rehabilitation care. I certainly was ready for us to get to rehab. We understood now that we were running a marathon and not a sprint, and we had a long, slow, but progressive road ahead.

The move to Shepherd Center was exciting—and scary. Everything about this entire process has had a scary side. I drove on ahead to get the paperwork ready so Bruce could be taken directly to his room. Being at Shepherd Center is so different than being an inpatient at a hospital. Hope is the pervading atmosphere there.

I was immediately given an appointment to meet with the Social Security Disabilities representative who came frequently to the hospital. I thought, "We're not going to need this." However, in the long run, we did. Everyone should have long-term disability insurance. It is not expensive, and this type of accident can happen too easily. We didn't have long-term disability insurance, but we should have. The employees at Shepherd Center guided us through every step of the Social Security Disability application and helped us adapt to Bruce's new life as the survivor of a brain injury.

When Bruce was brought in from the ambulance, he looked so helpless and weak. The nurses settled him in his bed, and he immediately fell asleep. Dr. Darryl Kaelin, the head of the Acquired Brain Injury floor, asked me, "What do you hope to gain from us?" I said, "Please don't send me home with a junkie. He is so addicted to morphine and Percocet right now." He assured me that Shepherd Center didn't deal with pain with morphine or other medications resulting in addiction. What a relief! I knew we were in the right place.

Bruce's abdomen was so distended that he looked like a bloated hippopotamus. Dr. Kaelin immediately asked about the size of his abdomen and then realized his intestines were blocked. Rachel asked if anyone had checked his bladder. They immediately went to work. His body was filling up with waste and urine.

A catheter was inserted to drain the bladder. Normally, the average bladder holds 400 cc of urine. They removed 1600 cc from him and had to use two bags to hold it all. No wonder Bruce was bloated so badly. Of course, the extra waste had been causing him excruciating pain for the past week, so the release really helped him relax and start feeling better. However, since his right side didn't function, he didn't know when his bladder was full. The nurses had to insert a catheter every four hours for the next five weeks. Talk about being regular and scheduled! This was not Bruce's favorite memory from Shepherd Center, but at least he didn't look pregnant anymore—and was not in pain.

The staff was getting Bruce in shape to begin therapy in three days. He was having a terrible time since he was also coming off the morphine, but when Monday arrived, he was ready. He had a great, determined, expectant attitude toward it all. The therapists worked him hard every day from 9 a.m. to 3 p.m., and he demonstrated strength, stamina, and pure grit.

Bruce's Thoughts

Shepherd Center! Our daughter, Rachel, was enjoying her job very much there and happened to be exactly what I needed. There are two types of brain injury: traumatic brain injuries

(TBI), which are caused by accidents of any kind, and acquired brain injuries (ABI), which are produced by the brain, such as a tumor or abscess. When Gabby Giffords, the senator from Arizona, was shot in the head, she had a traumatic brain injury.[1] She and I are testimonies to what can happen when a patient gets the right help quickly. If I had not received good care in the first six months, I do not believe I would be walking, talking, or writing this book today!

Not everyone who experiences a traumatic brain injury realizes the need to go to a specialized hospital for brain injuries. Bob Woodruff, the ABC news correspondent who was blown up by an IED in Iraq, definitely learned the importance of receiving specialized care for his brain injury. He returned to TV to deliver the news and to make people aware of what rehab treatment can accomplish.[2]

Getting care as early as possible is also vital. When Natasha Richardson, Liam Neeson's wife, fell during a beginner ski lesson in Canada, she thought she was fine; however, her headaches developed within hours, and she died three days later.[3] Any bump on the head should be checked out for a concussion or a more serious injury. A fractured skull is not readily detectable, but the damage from the swelling of the brain can be irreversible. I will be forever grateful for Laura's intervention and ability to get things moving on my behalf. She was a real trooper and did not give up on the possibility of getting me into Shepherd Center. I cannot imagine my life now without Shepherd Center.

---

[1] "Gabby Giffords' Remarkable Recovery," *ABC News,* November 4, 2011, http://abcnews.go.com/WNT/video/gabby-giffords-remarkable-recovery-14885317.

[2] "Bob Woodruff," *ABC News,* October 14, 2008, http://abcnews.go.com/WNT/story?id=127761.

[3] "Liam Neeson's wife, Natasha Richardson, Dies," *Belfast Telegraph,* March 19, 2009, http://www.belfasttelegraph.co.uk/entertainment/film-tv/news/liam-neesons-wife-natasha-richardson-dies-14232651.html.

Before heading for to this fine facility, I remember my final shot of morphine for the thirty-minute transfer trip. I was basically a vegetable and in need of some very quick and expert help. I remember rolling down the main hallway of Shepherd Center, but it was all such a blur. I only knew I was alive, and I needed help. I couldn't see well, but I could see that my room had color. Of course, anything that wasn't an ICU room looked beautiful to me.

That night turned out to be one of my worst nights in all of my time in any hospital. The doctors had taken me off of all the morphine. I pretty much was a junkie at that point, and I needed my shots. I also needed to have a bowel movement which I hadn't had in weeks. The body is a marvelous wonder, but when it starts to shut down, the process is painful. Not only was my leg hurting like it was on fire, but now I had a gastric nasal tube down my throat in order to pump all of the gas out of my stomach.

Dr. Kaelin had a great knowledge of pharmaceuticals. As he took me off the morphine, he knew I still needed some relief from the burning pain on my right side. The neurons in my brain were misfiring. My right side wasn't really hurt, but my brain was telling me it was. Dr. Kaelin immediately put me on Lyrica, which was a life saver.

Every morning, Agatha, my tech, would get me up for my shower. After five weeks with no shower, she was a welcome sight. She was small, feisty, and very loud, and every morning she would come in to say, "Good morning, Juicy Brucie!" That was the nickname she had given me since she was in charge of IC-ing my bladder every four hours for four weeks. (It has been four years since my surgery, and when I go to Shepherd Center now, she *still* calls me Juicy Brucie.) Agatha asked me each morning what my name was, where I was, and what day it was. I didn't always have the right answers. Her voice sounded like nails on a chalkboard as she forced me to get out of bed to get ready for breakfast and therapy. I sat naked in the wheelchair in the specially designed rehab shower and washed myself with my one good hand. Then I toweled off, which was not an easy thing to do while sitting in a wheelchair with limited mobility. I have a lot more respect now for people who are in wheelchairs.

After the shower, Agatha rolled me in front of the mirror to brush my teeth. I didn't really like looking at myself. I had lost weight and was bald. I felt like I was looking at someone else. Agatha gave me a toothbrush and helped me brush my teeth a little bit with my left hand. It was very difficult to do things with my left hand since I'm really right-handed. Agatha became the bright spot in my morning. Each day these activities became habits, and those habits became part of my daily routine, which in turn enabled me to get back into some type of functioning ability. Routine is so very important for the recovery of a person with a brain injury. It might interest you to know that I was in an adult diaper all this time, but don't feel sorry for me. I was just happy to have some sort of protection. The question was, "How long would I be dependent on Depends?"

I am leaving you with a gift—peace of mind and heart.
And the peace I give is a gift the world cannot give.
So don't be troubled or afraid.
John 14:27

Chapter 11

Progress at Last

Laura's Thoughts

UPDATE
Shepherd Center, February 12, 2008

Moving to Shepherd Center has been a wonderful experience—especially for Bruce. It has lifted his spirits, and he feels like he is making progress. The therapists specializing on speech, physical, occupational, and recreational needs. Bruce spends thirty to sixty minutes a day in each type of therapy. The physical therapy sessions have drained him, but also have strengthened him. He is able to move his right arm now—he can't control it, but he can move it. We are grateful for any advancement.

His eyesight is improving somewhat. He still has difficulty with blank spots. Please pray with us that his sight will be completely restored.

Bruce is known as Mr. Personality on the Brain Injury floor. He knows everyone by name and strikes up a conversation with all the patients. They may be semi-comatose and can't respond, but he talks to them like they can. He knows they can hear him, and he wants to give them something else to think about besides their situation. He has ministered and counseled with other patients' families. You can take the brain out of the preacher, but you can't take the preacher out of the brain!

Nate, a newlywed drill sergeant from Fort Benning, had an infection similar to Bruce's. He was in a coma for a month and left Shepherd Center a week after we arrived. His recuperation was a real encouragement to Bruce. His wife said they wanted to have kids, but she was glad they didn't have any before this happened to him. Bruce immediately asked if he could pray for them. As we all held hands together and Bruce prayed, Nate and his wife both cried. We don't know what happened to them after leaving Shepherd Center, but I remember the last infertile woman he prayed for now has five kids.

A wonderful Christian man, Dr. Kaelin reminded Bruce that we are to ask God to be a light unto our feet, not a floodlight looking out in the distance. He said God will light the path if we keep our focus on one step at a time. Such words of wisdom.

The speech therapist worked with Bruce a couple of times a day. The physical therapist taught him how to use his good leg and arm to move his wheelchair, and the occupational therapist worked with his eyesight and taught him to feed himself. When Bruce couldn't see the food on the plate, feeding himself was difficult. However, his sight gradually returned, and things moved forward. He had some blank spots in his vision, and we had to wait for progress as the swelling in the brain continued to diminish. The weakness in his right side was expected to strengthen. We were told that Bruce might walk with a cane when this was over. That would be a small price to pay for all he was going through.

Bruce's right side had been non-functional—with no movement or response to his mental commands. Then he moved the ends of his fingers and his thumb. The next day he could minimally move the arm itself. The doctor was ecstatic. Imagine what we felt. It's amazing how excited we got over something that we took so for granted in everyday life.

We had only been at Shepherd Center for a week, and already Bruce was sitting up and responding to therapy. He had come a long way from being a limp rag. A friend from Warner Robins, Georgia, where we used to live, had run a marathon that was very taxing. She won a medal for her efforts. As she presented the medal to him, she said, "When you walk out of this place, I want you to wear this medal to symbolize the marathon that you have won." We pinned it to his bulletin board at the foot of his bed so he could see it every day and press for the goal. This *was* a marathon he was running, and his medal was waiting for him.

Bruce was a Rancho VI by the time we arrived at Shepherd Center. This excellent scale of one through eight measures the progress of a brain injured person. The various levels, the patient's reactions, and the caregiver's response are explained in *The Rancho Levels of Cognitive Functioning* (see Appendix B). Having a "mild" head injury does not mean the person has "mild" problems. This type of injury can prevent someone from returning to work and can make family relationships a nightmare. Those who appear "normal" are sometimes those who suffer the most. They may look the same and talk the same—but they are very different.[4]

Valentine's Day fell during our first week at Shepherd Center. I gave Bruce a big, hairy, pink gorilla holding a sign that said, "I love you!" I moved it to his food table or the chair. It made him feel like he was never alone in the room. Agatha straightened Bruce's bed while he was in therapy every day. When he returned, he never knew where he would find the gorilla. Sometimes it was lying on the bed, or peeking out of the closet, or hiding somewhere else. It's funny what small efforts can bring joy.

---

[4]   Dr. Glen Johnson, *Traumatic Brain Injury Survival Guide,* June 25, 2010, http://www.tbiguide.com.

BRUCE'S THOUGHTS

The first time I saw Dr. Kaelin, I thought he looked like Doogie Howser with his young face and curly hair. He was very perceptive about brain injuries. Everything was a blur to me, so I do not really remember all the difficult moments. I thank God for my family, my wife, and all those wonderful nurses, techs, and doctors who helped to make my life better.

On my second day at Shepherd Center, I got my wheels. I had never pictured myself in a wheelchair before my surgery, but now it provided me some much wanted mobility. To get from the bed into the wheelchair, I was lifted by a Hoyer lift. Suspended from a motor in the ceiling over the bed, this strong net seat was put underneath me in the bed. Then all four corners of the net were lifted by this machine, raising me up like Superman. The first time I went up in the lift was kind of scary, especially since Laura was running it! The lift followed the ceiling track and carried me from over the bed to the wheelchair. I was then lowered into the chair. The netting stayed underneath me in the wheelchair so the process could be repeated in reverse when I was ready for the bed again.

I was then rolled to the end of the hallway and through some double doors. Without the use of my right leg or my right arm, I was unable to wheel myself, but I certainly enjoyed the ride. We were on our way to my first appointment with my physical therapist. Those of us who have endured PT also call it pain and torture.

My physical therapist for the next five weeks was a tall, rather lean, and sturdy person named Margaret. I called her *Hot Lips* because of Margaret on the TV show M*A*S*H, but she was too young to know what I was talking about. The first thing she wanted me to do was sit up straight on the bench. You would think that would be easy, but I was like a rag doll. I fell over sideways and could not sit straight. The brain injury had definitely affected my balance. Dr. Kaelin asked me to close my eyes and touch my nose with my left hand, which I did very easily. Then he asked me to touch my right hand to my nose. I had no movement on my right side and couldn't figure out where my nose was. It was obvious that I needed a lot of help.

Having a brain injury was like going down the rabbit hole of *Alice in Wonderland.* Clocks were oblong and strange, and numbers were a complete enigma to me. I did not know why I didn't understand numbers w, but they were a complete mystery. The left parietal lobe, which deals with math, verbal, executive, and decision-making functions, was the injured part of my brain. Even words and spelling were completely gone. Therefore, sitting up was about all I could do at the moment, and it took all of my concentration to sit for one minute and not fall over.

During those first few days at Shepherd Center, I had some hallucinations—probably because I was being weaned off of morphine. The sweet nurse, Vera, who came in at night to pray with me and sing lullabies, appeared at my door in the middle of the night. She looked like a monster sticking out her long tongue tauntingly at me. Terrified, I screamed and told her to get out and never come back. My brain was definitely not working very well. I could totally relate to King Nebuchadnezzar in the Bible who wandered aimlessly in the wilderness for seven years before regaining his mind. I'm so glad I was not alone without my caregiver and my therapists.

After a few days, I became quite good at maneuvering my wheelchair. My useless right arm laid on the armrest while my right leg was propped up on the footrest. However, as I gradually got stronger, my left arm and leg made up for the lack of movement on my right side. Of course, I went in circles a lot as I propelled myself with my foot and hand, but I went as fast as I could. The nurse asked, "What in the world are you doing, Mr. Allen?" I answered, "I'm going to get well as fast as

I can, so I'm getting some exercise." Falling into bed for a nap that afternoon was a welcome relief.

So be strong and courageous! Do not
be afraid and do not panic
before them. For the Lord your God will
personally go ahead of you.
He will neither fail you nor abandon you.
Deuteronomy 31:6

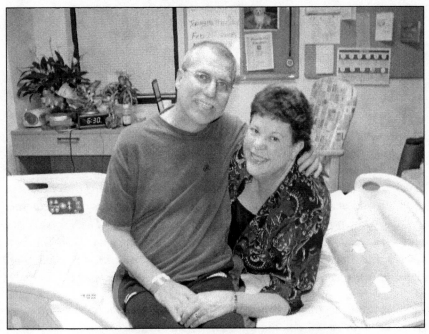

Sitting up—sort of—at Shepherd Center

Chapter 12

For the Caregiver

LAURA'S THOUGHTS

UPDATE
Shepherd Center, February 21, 2008

Slowly, but surely. So many things we take for granted—moving of the fingers or hand, bending the leg at the knee, telling time on the clock, shifting from the bed to the wheelchair and back, and standing—in a frame that teaches someone to walk again. These were all moments for rejoicing this week for Bruce. The therapists and nurses (particularly one night nurse we know very well!) are amazing at Shepherd Center. The atmosphere here is one of anticipation, encouragement, and hope. Everyone is so nice, and we do feel like we are part of a larger family.

Please continue to pray for Bruce. His bowels and bladder have been sluggish to get "back in the game," and this causes severe pain at times.

We were back to the basics—the *real* basics. Bruce was learning how to be around people again (to which he adapted very quickly), sit up, feed himself, get dressed, walk, speak—everything that a typical two-year-old should learn. Bruce was suffering from ataxia—the brain's inability to remember what it is supposed to do. Everything had to be reprogrammed since much of the data had been erased. However, Bruce was up for the challenge and was a real trooper.

The brain injury survivor must *want* to get better and be willing to do whatever it takes in therapy to see results. The person must be encouraged that he can, in fact, do whatever it takes, but he can't look at the big picture or he will be overwhelmed and possibly give up.

This is where the role of the caregiver is so important. Often caregivers feel like they should be doing whatever they can to help bring the person along. In reality, at this stage, "bringing the person along" is the role of the therapist. The caregiver's role is to encourage, praise, comfort, and love the patient. This will help build the patient's will to succeed. When Bruce first said "pencil" when shown the picture, fireworks went off in the room! We praised him. That might sound childish, but remember, we were working with someone who was like a preschooler learning everything from square one. We had praised our children for the smallest accomplishments when they were young. This was just as important—if not more so.

The brain injury didn't only happen to your loved one. It happened to you and your family, too. You will need time to heal emotionally. Things have been turned upside down in all areas of your life. You will need to embrace that and accept it to be able to move forward. The cycle of grief that presents itself as a result of a negative event coming into your life goes through variations of the following stages:

- Shock stage: Initially feeling paralyzed at hearing the bad news

- Denial stage: Trying to avoid the inevitable

- Anger stage: Frustrated outpouring of bottled-up emotion

- Bargaining stage: Seeking in vain for a way out

- Depression stage: Finally realizing the inevitable

- Testing stage: Seeking realistic solutions

- Acceptance stage: Finally finding the way forward[5]

As the caregiver, you need to work through this cycle at your own pace to deal with all aspects of the grief you are feeling. If you don't, you will get stuck in one stage, and that definitely won't be healthy for you or for the recovery of your loved one who is going to be depending on you. As you deal with each level in the cycle, you will move forward and finally spin out of the circle to be able to function as you need to.

A major lesson that I learned very early on in this experience was to take the phrase "what if" out of my vocabulary. What if he never walks again? What if he doesn't regain his sight? What if he doesn't speak again? I could go on and on. However, what does that accomplish except to feed fear and anxiety? Thoughts like this would only drive me crazy—and wear me out. It is unhealthy mentally, emotionally and physically. How would my fear and anxiety help Bruce? Sometimes I would slip back into "leaning on my own understanding" (Proverbs 3:5), but in those times, I would stand up straight and once again tighten my grip on God's hand.

Take care of yourself as the caregiver. Get plenty of rest and eat well. Sometimes that means making yourself get out of the hospital to go for a walk or to take a nap. Do something for yourself. Get your nails done, have a massage, exercise to work out the stress if you can. You need to clear your mind to be a better caregiver. The hospital staff is there to care for your loved one. You will have plenty of opportunity—and little time to rest—when you take him or her home (see Appendices C and D).

---

[5] Elisabeth Kubler-Ross, *On Death and Dying* (New York: Simon & Schuster/ Touchstone, 1969).

BRUCE'S THOUGHTS

The simple activities—sitting in a wheelchair or upright on the bench—became small victories! They were great achievements to me since all I had been doing for five weeks was lying in bed and getting morphine shots.

My therapists worked together as a team to ensure my progress. When I stood in the standing frame for ten minutes, several of the therapists applauded and said, "Wow, you really did great! This is awesome. You are doing wonderfully. Keep up the good work." I can't tell you how encouraging it was to hear those words even though I really didn't understand everything that was going on around me. I knew that they were pleased and smiling, so that made me proud of myself. Laura was *really* pleased. She did not go to therapy every day; in fact, she was told not to come so that I could focus on what the therapist told me to do. I also had an occupational therapist who helped me regain some of my executive functions. Maybe I could go back to work soon. Praise and encouragement from my therapists and my caregiver were invaluable to my mental attitude.

Sometimes it's hard for a caregiver to communicate with a brain injured person. You may have to play charades to communicate even the slightest thought. Just being there is the most important thing you can do. Don't try to help with therapy—that's what the therapists are for. Trust the therapists— they know what they are doing. Love on your patient—your husband, child, or wife—and give encouragement. Celebrate the small victories—raising an arm, speaking a word, or walking for the first time.

Laura did many things for me that meant so much: cutting my fingernails and getting my hair cut so it wasn't matted. Cutting my fingernails and toenails was a big deal to me. I felt like my nails were growing really long, like bird claws. It felt so good emotionally to get myself fixed up a bit. That may sound crazy, but that's the way the brain injured person thinks. Laura also gave me foot massages with lotion almost daily. She didn't keep it up after a year or so, but it was certainly appreciated in the hospital! Most important were the acts that related to everyday living. I couldn't shave myself, so she brought an electric shaver and did it for me. I eventually learned to shave myself. That was awesome. Feeding your loved one is a good opportunity to talk about everyday things even though it may be a one-sided conversation. My family came to visit on the weekends which lifted my spirits. Too many people at once can be overwhelming, but two at a time is OK. Nothing can substitute for family.

A patient told us that her mother would lie down beside her on the bed to let her know she was there. The little things mean so much. My wife came every afternoon after my therapy, and I looked forward to her visits to see what she had brought me. Whether it was a magazine, food, candy, or a music CD, her small gifts added spice to my day full of therapy. She always brought a surprise.

Shepherd Center had a beautiful place called the Garden where family members could take their patient outside. One day as Laura wheeled me out to the Garden for some sunshine, Rachel came through the gate with our dog, Princess! Princess jumped into my lap in the wheelchair and slurped all over my face. (Slurping was a good word to describe the moment.) She was as happy to see me again as I was her. It was nice to be outside with my dog. Pet therapy is great. For people who like animals, there is nothing better—except family.

> Come to me, all of you who are weary
> and carry heavy burdens,
> and I will give you rest. Take my yoke upon you.
> Let me teach you, because I am humble and gentle at heart,
> and you will find rest for your souls.
> Matthew 11:28–29

Pet Therapy with Princess

Chapter 13

Aphasia

Laura's Thoughts

UPDATE
Shepherd Center, February 18, 2008

Bruce's speech is greatly improved. When he gets stuck on a word, the speech therapists are teaching him to thumb through his mental thesaurus to find another word. They told him to sing a word or a song to get his point across if he is having difficulty. I hope this singing phase passes quickly. It's also very interesting how Scripture always comes to him perfectly—"thy word have I hid in my heart."

"Laura, you know that thing that we do?"
"What thing?"
"When we cook outside."
"You mean, roast hotdogs?"
"No, sometimes we use chicken."
"You mean when we use the grill?"
"Yes, let's grill tonight!"

Seven sentences to pinpoint the word "grill." An hour later, or the next day, or a month later, the word "grill" may spring readily to his lips. Finding the right words to say is a common problem for brain injury survivors. It is more than forgetting a person's name. It involves searching for the word, picturing the object, and still not finding the word in the mental file cabinet to express the thought. This is called aphasia.

The general public has never heard of aphasia. The difficulties of aphasia are often misinterpreted as signs that the person is mentally retarded. Although a person with aphasia can have difficulty retrieving words and names, memories of situations, appointments, and people as well as general knowledge remains relatively intact. The ability to express some ideas and thoughts through language is disrupted. Improvement is a slow process that can take years or even decades. While the problem gradually improves, the individual and family must learn other ways of communicating.

When Bruce tells his brain injury story, he often starts with "I had a hysterectomy." That always brings a laugh. Of course, he means he had hemorrhoid surgery, but he can't remember that word, and the next word in his mental file cabinet is apparently hysterectomy.

I mentioned earlier that when Rachel's heating element went out, he said, "We've got to fix her elephant." If a person says the wrong word and he can laugh at himself, the situation can be alright. However, if he can't find any word at all and stares blankly, it can be quite embarrassing for both the person and the listener. Understanding is all you can offer at the moment.

Aphasia can cause brain injury survivors to say "right" when they mean "left," "yes" when they mean "no," write "23" when they mean "32," and can impede mental processes such as adding numbers. When Bruce is tired or fatigued, he exhibits more signs of aphasia. In that condition, finding the right words often becomes difficult. Sometimes a nonsense word will come out. When listening to a speech or movie, he may lose the first few words of dialogue, and then the whole thought is lost. Processing the words in his mind is slow. How many times has he asked, "What did he say? What did he say?" He often misses the first few words. His hearing is fine—his processing is not.

Another interesting aspect of aphasia is that Bruce can pull some of the strangest, longest, and largest words out of his vocabulary file cabinet. He says them like they are very common and uses them correctly. He was looking for the word "extra" to use in a sentence and instead said, "Would you hand me that superfluous pencil on the table?" I had to look it up in the dictionary to understand what he was saying.

Recently Bruce was telling me about his cousin who was ill and was planning to go to a specialist. The conversation went like this:

"My cousin is sick."
"Oh, I'm sorry to hear that."
"In a few weeks she's going to, uh, you know..."
"No, I don't know. She's going to what?"
"She's going where...she's going where she's going."
"And where's that?"
"Oh, you know—where your dad said everyone should go."
"You mean Mayo Clinic?"
"Yes, yes, she's going to Mayo Clinic."
"Why would she go to Minneapolis in December?"
"Well, she's going to Florida."
"Oh, to the Mayo Clinic in Jacksonville?"
"Yes, my cousin is going to the Mayo Clinic in Jacksonville, Florida."

I'm worn out after a mental workout like this, but it keeps my mind sharp just trying to keep his mind sharp.

BRUCE'S THOUGHTS

I didn't know what a speech therapist was until I had been assigned one, and, boy, did I get a great one. Not only was she smart, but she was also pretty. As we sat across the table from one another, she would have me look at items in a box. As she held up a pencil, she asked, "Do you know what this is?" I knew in my mind what it was, but I couldn't think of the word no matter how hard I tried. She said, "Pencil," and then I was able to say "pencil" back, but that's all I could say. She would go to the next item in the box, a paperclip, and she would say, "Do you know what this is?" Again, I couldn't think of the word, and I'd shake my head no. When she said "paperclip," I filed it away in my mental file cabinet of words, gradually rebuilding my vocabulary. As she held up picture cards of a house or a car, again she would ask what it was. Again, I couldn't say the name. My brain would not process what I saw in order to say the word. For a man who was a preacher and had dealt with words constantly, this was a new experience. I realized it would take hours, days, and months—even years—of therapy to fill up my "word file cabinet." However, it is amazing what the human spirit can do.

My speech therapist asked me to name animals starting with A in the alphabet. She was asking a lot—and I only had one minute to do it. I would have to remember the alphabet first. Then I'd have to process which animal started with that letter, and then speak the name. I really didn't realize what goes into the entire process of saying or doing things until I couldn't say or do them. I was able to name three animals in a minute. You'd think that would have been a breeze since I knew so much about Noah's ark, but that knowledge was of no help. She asked me to name the colors: green, blue, red, purple, etc. For a person with a doctorate in theology, not knowing the names of colors or numbers was a very humbling experience. It was like starting over in pre-school. I didn't know anything.

Bob Woodruff explained that, after his traumatic brain injury in Iraq, aphasia was very much a part of his everyday speaking. He could understand a word, but he couldn't always say it. When he woke up in the hospital, he couldn't name any states or the words for hamburger or egg sandwich. Nouns were the most difficult to recall. Once he said, "I feel one thousand dollars better today." He intended to say "one thousand percent," but he mixed up dollars, measurements, miles and inches.[6] I had the same experience with referring to numbers. I mentioned to a friend that we had paid $50,000 for our 1997 Honda Civic. Obviously, I was a little off—in more ways than one!

I enjoy hearing a good joke or funny story, but don't expect me to remember it. I used to be a pretty good joke teller. Now when I get to the punch line, I turn to Laura and ask, "How did that story end?" Hopefully, she remembers. If not, we all laugh at how the many ways it could have ended. It is an effort to read a book or the newspaper, and I usually need a nap after attempting this exercise. As my eyes scan the lines, the words sometimes get out of order or mixed up. Often I have to read each word individually until the reading flows smoothly again. It helps to hold a piece of paper below each line to keep my eyes from getting lost in all the words on the page. Naturally, it takes me longer to read a book, but I'm not in a race.

I have learned to "talk around" a word. It's kind of like playing charades. If I can't think of the word I want, I describe it. For "telephone" I might say, "You punch the keys, you talk to people on it, it has 'apps.'" Somebody eventually will get what I'm trying to say.

Give people with aphasia time to speak, and do not finish their sentences unless you are asked. Be sensitive to background noise; turn off competing sounds such as radios or TV's when possible.[7] Be open to using other means of communication like, you know—when you use crayons—or a pencil—on a piece of paper—making marks—that look like—you know, uh...

---

[6] Todd Plitt, "Struggle for Words Frustrates Woodruff," *USA Today*, February 24, 2008, http://www.usatoday.com/news/health/2008-02-24-bob-woodruff_N.htm.

[7] *National Aphasia Association*, 2009, http://www.aphasia.org.

Chapter 14

It Is What It Is

LAURA'S THOUGHTS

UPDATE
Shepherd Center, February 26, 2008

Yesterday the doctor told me Bruce had turned a corner. The therapists had taken him to Blockbuster that morning for an outing to experience the real world. It wasn't quite Starbucks, he said, but it was a beautiful day outside to go rent a movie. However, I didn't think that warranted a comment about "turning a corner" in his recovery.

But then <u>today</u> happened. As his nurse said, "Bruce had an <u>awesome day</u>." Here's what transpired:

- *He didn't have any pain medication—first day since 1/2/08.*

- *He didn't need to have any Gas-X for abdominal pain—first day since 1/25/08.*

- *He felt the "urge" and used the commode three times—first time since 1/7/08.*

- *He learned to stand and pivot from the bed to the wheelchair—he doesn't use the slide board anymore.*

And then (drum roll, please):

- *Bruce walked today!*—*Using a walker on wheels, he walked the perimeter of a forty-food by eighty-foot room, putting that very weak right leg out, and then the left, etc., until he made it all the way around the room. The therapists working with other patients watched as he covered a distance that was unbelievable and cheered when he finished.*

This has been a busy, tiring, invigorating week for Bruce. His eyesight seems to be slowly improving—he has about 80% back. His speech is slowly improving—when he doesn't try to talk too fast.

Bruce was visiting with a friend and said that he knew God wasn't finished with him yet. He was excited to see what kind of ministry is going to come out of all this. We know God has been in control all along, and God is controlling the therapy now and in the days ahead. Bruce's positive attitude of determination and will-power has been amazing—it's a God-given attribute. He calls the other patients his congregation and really meets their needs as he talks with them and their families.

A major milestone is that his bladder rejoined the body team last night as a functioning member. That was becoming a real concern for Bruce, but once again, God let the "floodgates of blessings flow." (Please forgive the really bad pun—I couldn't help myself.)

Please keep praying for Bruce. Of course, his right side continues to need strengthening, as does his walking. He still stumbles over some words when he talks too fast—but so do I. (What do you think that means?) He will move on to the next level of rehab on March 20 when we transfer to outpatient therapy, which will last from 8 a.m. to 2:30 p.m., five days a week for twenty weeks. The great strides we have seen in his recovery so far are definitely answers to prayer. The doctors and therapists say he is the star of the unit, and it is a pleasure to work with someone who has such drive and determination to do whatever they ask.

Each night after supper, Bruce makes his rounds to visit the other patients who can respond to him in some way. It is a joy to see their faces light up when he rolls into their rooms, especially since they only exhibited sadness when we first met them. He visits with them, says some encouraging words about their progress, and moves on to the next room. He always loved hospital visitation as a pastor, but I never thought I'd see him enjoy it this much.

The physical therapist put electrodes on Bruce's limp right arm and, with a remote control glove, made his arm move around. His hand could make a fist, and he could raise his arm above shoulder height. However, the therapist was making all that happen. Bruce had no control over the movement. It was really fascinating. She was sending electronic messages to the brain to remind it what it was supposed to be doing. Later that evening, Bruce started showing me what he could do with his arm and hand. It was all those same movements, but he was controlling the commands with his own mind. Apparently the therapist got her message through. The brain is amazing—and so were these therapists and their equipment. His limp right leg responded the next week to the same stimulus. There was only very slight movement in the leg, but then it responded as the arm did. His right side continued to strengthen and improve little by little. The therapist made him sit on his good hand and fold towels with the weak arm and hand. I told her I appreciated her training him to fold laundry for when he comes home.

Bruce had what the therapists call a floppy foot. His brain didn't know to hold it in a normal position so he could walk. A foot brace was fit inside his right shoe to strengthen the right ankle. It made such a difference in his ability to walk. He also slept with a bi-valve, which looked like a removable leg cast. It kept his foot in a walking position while he slept so the brain would hopefully remember that it is supposed to be that way.

A hanging drip of Bruce's antibiotic to kill the brain infection had been given two times a day since January 7. When Bruce had his last IV, we passed another milestone—ten weeks on two IVs a day. That should have killed every infection that ever lived in his body, and apparently it did.

The occupational therapists took Bruce on a shopping spree to the CVS Pharmacy across the street from the hospital to maneuver in the store, pick out a few things, and then pay for them. He said it was really weird how people looked at someone in a wheelchair. Of course, the fact that he had a three-inch by four-inch dent in the back of his head wouldn't have anything to do with drawing attention, would it? (The doctor said he would put a plastic plate in Bruce's skull in June to cover the section that had been removed.)

Bruce ventured out on another shopping spree to CVS, and then the therapists took Bruce to a sub shop for lunch. He said reentry into the real world was strange and a little scary. While in CVS, he managed to walk in the aisles with the walker. That was not even thinkable two weeks before.

As we continued through physical therapy and speech therapy, as well as occupational, cognitive, and recreational therapies, Bruce improved and relearned how to live. Sometimes the improvement was rapid, and other times it was slow. If I had dwelt on the "What If's," I would have been wasting a lot of my time and energy on issues that later were resolved. Recovery is one step at a time—and each step is usually forward. We may go forward one step and then back two steps, but the next time will be three steps forward. As humans, we are conditioned to expect things to progress in a systematic, organized, and quick way. I was always a "get 'er done, do it now, fix-it" kind of person who thought that the fastest way to a resolution was the best way. However, the brain heals at its own pace, so we might as well relax, watch for the signs of improvement as they happen, and let nature run its course. As our neurosurgeon said, "It takes as long as it takes." Patience was a hard lesson for me to learn, but over the past four years, patience has translated into smelling the roses along the way, living life to its fullest, and taking the relaxing times to be with family and friends.

"It is what it is." I never really did like that phrase. I thought it was redundant, a bit trite, and self-defeating like, "I've given up." After entering the world of brain injuries, however, I changed my tune. Each day was, and continues to be, just what it is. Today Bruce doesn't know that a stick with a point is a pencil. Soon, however, he will readily recognize it is a pencil—and say so.

Moving forward through rehabilitation is slow but progressive. Being fed by someone else advances to holding a spoon on his own. Hopefully, he will eventually feed himself. It may take three weeks to make the complete transition, but it is an accomplishment. Each step is what it is. The next step forward is what it is. Keeping the focus on the here and now keeps us from getting ahead of ourselves and focusing on the What Ifs.

Bruce slept twelve hours a night along with daytime cat naps. I thought that maybe he was regressing or slipping into a coma when I wasn't looking—as if my looking made any difference at all. I learned that the brain heals when it sleeps. The neurons that have been misfiring or not firing at all are searching for new pathways through the brain to get their respective jobs done. The brain has an amazing ability to remap itself and to find new pathways to accomplish its tasks particularly in the early stages. Sleep is when this rewiring takes place. So, sleep on, brother!

I watched with amazement as the physical therapists gradually took Bruce from sitting like a limp rag to actually standing. It was miraculous! It took two weeks, but it was worth seeing every moment move in the direction of eventually standing. After four weeks at Shepherd Center, I was shocked to see a man walking down the hall in front of me with a therapist on either side. All patients wear a wide belt around their waists, borrowing stability from the therapists who hold on to it. Margaret, Bruce's main physical therapist, was one of those holding on to the belt. As she looked back at me, she said, "Don't say anything or it will throw him off." Then I realized it was Bruce slowly walking down the hall with a walker and the two therapists in tow. Talk about rejoicing! It was hard to heed Margaret's warning, but I certainly didn't want to mess up his balance. That was a real victory day. "It is what it is," and it was good!

BRUCE'S THOUGHTS

Neurons in the brain send impulses to one another to facilitate memory, thought, speech, and movement. When an injury occurs, the neuron connections are disconnected either temporarily or permanently. The brain has the amazing ability to rewire itself and make new pathways for the neurons to continue their assigned duties, which is called plasticity.

In my case, the left parietal lobe was damaged, and, therefore, all of my numbers were gone as well as my management and executive skills. I didn't know what a two or a six was. It didn't matter that I couldn't add or subtract them. I didn't know what numbers were. This is very hard to understand for people who have never had a brain injury. Over the past three years, however, my brain has managed to rewire itself enabling those neurons to reconnect. The pathways of the brain facilitate billions and billions of neurons. The brain is actually like a computer. In fact, I've been told that one square inch of the brain contains more neuronal connections then there are stars in the Milky Way. I'm not sure who counted the number of stars in the Milky Way, but it is a lot.

Through plasticity, the brain is able to file various words and information in different file drawers. If I can't find the word I'm looking for, the brain will open another drawer or rewire itself through a different pathway to help me locate another word. Not all connections can be restored, but the brain tries very hard to restore itself.

Music is an excellent tool to help a brain injury survivor find the missing word. During speech therapy, if I were trying to think of the word "star," the therapist would ask if I knew the song, "Twinkle, Twinkle, little _____?" I still couldn't find the word, but once she started singing the song, I joined her. Then the word automatically filled in the blank. It might take a couple of tries, but I finally filed away "star" in my new vocabulary drawer, and it would be there the next time I needed it. Music therapy is amazing. The music side of the brain is located in a different area than the language section. As I sang, I was able to access a different part of the memory that, in turn, helped restock the words in my word bank. It is fascinating to watch the brain heal itself.

I had to reteach myself the words that had always been readily at hand—and I succeeded little by little. Seeing the small victories of recall gave me the determination to strive for more successes. Repetition and an increasing vocabulary brought me back to being a "talking machine."

Somewhere along the way I began to see some positive results with my right side deficits. My right leg and my right arm responded to the electrotherapy. My hands began to move ever so slightly. I remember the day when I could actually feel a slight touch to my right arm. It was truly a great day. As I worked hard in therapy, I understood that I had to stay active and keep trying. I know of a brain injury survivor who said that even after nine years, she was still experiencing some improvements with her deficits. It has taking me four years so far, and I am still seeing improvements. As I said before, life is a rehab center. Every activity brings me closer to getting back to "normal"—whatever that is.

The first time I stood up in the standing machine was exhilarating. Every time I stood for a certain length of time, my blood pressure lowered, and I felt faint. I gradually was able to stand without feeling faint. This seems like a small victory, but I still remember the day I stood upright for several minutes. It was extremely exciting.

Simple tasks weren't so simple for me. I was asked to put pegs in holes and coordinate their colors. My eyesight was slightly improving, but it was not nearly back to normal. I could barely see the colors, much less the pegs. However, as I kept on trying, my skill improved over the weeks of therapy. In the business world, it is said that your attitude determines your altitude. It is also true in real life—especially when you have a disability. The amount of success experienced during therapy is directly proportionate to my willingness to give it my all. As I pushed and strived to take that small step, my attitude was everything. By maintaining a positive attitude, I was more likely to accomplish my maximum potential.

When I wasn't in therapy, I watched a lot of TV. One of my favorite afternoon shows was about little people—dwarfs and midgets. I was intrigued as they adapted their lives in every way so they could function in a world of big people. One of the boys had eight surgeries on his leg to correct a malformed knee. With amazement, I watched and was encouraged as he did his therapy. He gave me hope to face another day of "pain and torture."

As a brain injury survivor, I lived in the moment instead of feeling sorry for myself. I'm afraid most outside observers have the misconception that patients who experience a brain injury are immediately very distressed, worried about the future, and frustrated. For me, my existence was quite the opposite. I had no concept of time or life's situations outside of my room. I knew I was in the hospital, but beyond that, I lived for whatever was happening at the time. If dinner was brought, I ate. If I was tired, I slept. If the aides took me to therapy, I wanted to do whatever my therapists told me to do to the best of whatever ability I had. I didn't have the capacity to think about things that concerned people in the outside world. In recreational therapy, I made dish gardens, painted rocks with the symbol of my favorite college football team, and made art. I loved it. It worked my brain and awakened my "artsy" side. This therapy was different than the pain of physical therapy. It takes all kinds of therapy to recover from a brain injury.

He gives power to the weak and strength to the powerless.
Even youths will become weak and tired,
and young men will fall in exhaustion.

But those who trust in the Lord will find new strength.
They will soar high on wings like eagles.
They will run and not grow weary.
They will walk and not faint.
Isaiah 40:29–31

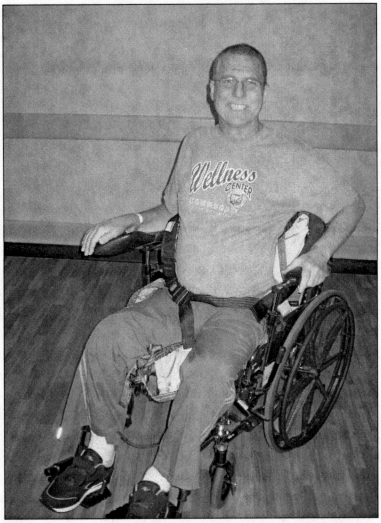

The Buzz Cut

Chapter 15

Depression and Anger

LAURA'S THOUGHTS

Depression and anger are very real parts of the brain injury survivor's recovery. Some people awaken angry from their accident. Others cry constantly. Some do both. When the brain was tossed about, emotions and other areas of functioning were scrambled around. The swelling of the brain in the first few days and weeks causes responses that were not part of the person before.

One survivor had never cursed. After his work-related accident, he cursed like a sailor. His wife was naturally very disturbed by this and took it very personally. She told me, "I can't live with this new person." I assured her that if she waited a few days or weeks until the swelling went down, there was a good chance that he would stop. Two weeks later, she excitedly told me that he didn't curse anymore, and she was so relieved.

A teenager, who was in a car wreck, constantly argued and yelled profanity every moment that he could no matter where he was. It was very disturbing to his family, who thought this would be part of their lives forever. After three weeks, he stopped.

Depression is also a normal spin-off from a brain injury, and understandably so. The doctor often prescribes an antidepressant so the patient doesn't become despondent and adversely affect his therapy. When he was experiencing the extreme abdominal pain, Bruce experienced some depression on his second day at Shepherd Center. After the pain was taken care of, the depression remained. Dr. Kaelin prescribed Paxil. It worked wonders and helped him move on through therapy with gusto. There are so many types of antidepressants, and one may work better than another. It is worth it to find the right medication for each individual.

Anger is a whole 'nother animal! The unaffected brain has the ability to "gate" life's experiences. We can be approached by a situation and feel the tension rising. We can decide to stop the discussion when we reach a seven on the anger scale so it doesn't escalate to a full-blown rage. The brain injury survivor doesn't have that "gating" ability. He can experience calm in his life, and then when he feels threatened, frustrated, or frightened, he can go from a one to a ten in an instant and explode uncontrollably. When the gating mechanism doesn't kick in, he feels an eruption of emotion before he can recognize what is happening—and it's too late.

Anger after a head injury is quite different than "normal" anger. This type of anger tends to have a quick "on" and a quick "off." The person can be in a good mood until something small irritates him, and he suddenly gets very angry. This anger doesn't seem to last. The person can be angry for a few minutes, and then quickly stop being angry when someone changes the topic of conversation.

At Shepherd Center one evening, Rachel and I were in Bruce's room. He wanted to watch a certain TV show, but it wasn't on that night. All of a sudden, he started screaming and threatening us. Rachel and I walked out of the room and stood in the hallway until we—and he—could calm down. From her nursing experience with brain injuries, Rachel told me to wait about ten minutes, and he would return to normal, but to let him calm down alone. It worked. After ten minutes, we went back in his room, and he was as sweet as ever—as if he didn't even know the explosion had happened.

Not being able to gate emotions can continue for years after recovery. When Bruce took Princess to the vet two years after his injury, the receptionist said he had to fill out a long information sheet. He couldn't write with his right hand, and his left hand-writing was illegible. He was frustrated and said he couldn't fill out the form. Then she said the credit card would not go through. I had failed to tell him that I had cancelled that card and was now using another one. He exploded with frustration because he couldn't fill out the form, and didn't know how else to pay. He couldn't solve the problem, and he was trying so hard to live a normal life. He phoned me, and I asked to speak to the lady. I apologized and explained the situation to her. Something like this had never happened before to him, but I certainly was going to guard against it in the future.

Bruce didn't want to ever go back to the vet's because of the extremely frustrating experience. However, I told him we would go together the next time because he needed to have a positive experience at the vet. We returned a year later—together. It was much better for him. The same lady quietly asked me how Bruce was doing. I was happy to tell her that he was doing *much* better.

The role of a caregiver never stops. You may have long stretches where things seem to be rolling along fine, but you never know when the gating won't work and an explosion will happen.

BRUCE'S THOUGHTS

One of the things I noticed immediately after my brain injury was that anger and emotions were right on the surface. It didn't take much to set off one or the other. Sometimes I would cry uncontrollably. Sometimes I would get extremely angry very quickly. Sometimes I would simply be depressed.

Depression is not something that you can think your way out of with positive thinking. As a minister, I used to believe that if I memorized enough verses about having faith and looked to God, I would be able to overcome any type of emotional depression. However, once I had a brain injury, I learned that it was not quite that easy. Dr. Kaelin gave me Paxil, which stimulates the neuronal connections and helps the brain to rewire itself. It's not just a matter of overcoming depression; it's also a matter of putting the right oil into the machinery, so it can function and run smoothly. Brains need certain chemicals in order to work properly. With a brain injury, everything is messed up, and some help may be needed. The antidepressant certainly took away the anxiety so I could function better in rehab.

When anger comes on me, it's not typical anger. When I become stressed, the anger instantly takes over. I cannot control my emotions. When the brain gets jumbled up, everything is displaced for a while until the swelling goes down. Quick anger and cursing can be two very unexpected byproducts of brain surgery. Usually, cursing and anger don't last long, but they definitely do happen. I don't normally curse, but I did on a couple of occasions when I was very frustrated.

I couldn't feed myself, and on one particular day, my stepmother, Faye, was waiting to feed me. Unfortunately, the lunch tray was very late that day, not arriving until 1:30pm. I was starving. A Kennestone therapist who wanted to see how I was progressing bounced into my room, pulled my newly delivered tray away from the bed, and said, "We are going to do your therapy now." I told her, in no uncertain terms, "I'm not doing therapy now. I'm going to eat my lunch." It was a battle between her printed schedule and my stomach. When she insisted that I was going to do therapy, I exploded and said, "Get the @%*& # out of my room and don't come back! I'm not doing therapy. I want to eat my lunch, and @#$%&, leave me alone!"

Of course, being a minister, I don't talk that way. It was somewhat disconcerting to my family to hear those words come out of my mouth (although my stepmother thought it was pretty funny). I did eat my lunch, and the therapist didn't come back to bother me that day. The fact that I told the therapist to never come back probably had something to do with it. I just wanted to eat my lunch in peace, and I hoped she understood.

With brain injuries, people often have gating issues and can say a variety of things that are quite unexpected and inappropriate. As Rachel, Laura, and I were enjoying dinner at Applebee's after I was released from Shepherd Center, a very buxom waitress came to take our order. It was hard to not notice how well-endowed she was. Without gating abilities, I may say whatever comes to mind and embarrass myself and everyone around. As the waitress started to take our order, she dropped her pen to the floor. She bent over next to me to retrieve it, saying, "I'm sorry." I responded, "Well, I'm not. I enjoyed watching you bend over to pick up your pen. You can do that anytime!" The waitress turned red, Laura and Rachel were shocked, but I didn't know I had said anything unusual. However, I certainly heard about it when we got home.

After completing my official rehab, I wanted to do "normal" things. I tried to back our boat trailer into the garage, but I couldn't manage to control where it was going. I got very angry at my wife—I was going into a rage. When an experience like this happens, I simply have to back away and go for a walk. This approach is called "taking a time out." When I feel that I am going to explode, I walk away. The more I use a time out, the more I learn to control my feelings or hold back the flood of emotion. "Time out" is a good thing. The problem is that the explosion happens so unexpectedly that I am stunned by it, too. Gaining control to take a walk and cool down is not easy. However, it only takes five to ten minutes to emotionally return to the pre-rage state. The person you are with has to know what is happening or real damage can be unintentionally caused to your relationship. Because of this uncontrollable reaction to stress, going back to work is impossible for me, in my opinion.

A brain injured friend of mine was in a bad car wreck and suffered a severe brain injury (is there any other kind?). Even now, two years after the wreck, he still can go into a rage. One day he actually threw a chair across the room. That was not his nature, but it happened when his anger exploded. Another friend tried to hit his wife with a glass coffeepot when his anger rose to a high level. Brain injury survivors know they have done something they have no control over. It is embarrassing and disturbing for them. Their families must exercise a lot of understanding as they work through this issue (see Appendix E).

Chapter 16

Leaving Shepherd Center for Pathways

Laura's Thoughts

UPDATE
Shepherd Center/Pathways, March 15, 2008

Bruce is ready to leave Shepherd Center and move on to Pathways—for outpatient therapy which will last from 8 a.m. to 2:30 p.m., five days a week, for twenty weeks. We will be able to stay at home, and Bruce will go to Pathways for rehab while I am at work. The great strides we have seen in his recovery so far are definitely answers to prayer. As he wheeled out of the hospital, he wore the marathon medal that he had to be given. He had won the good race—so far.

Boy, do I miss those nurses who got him anything he wanted when he wanted it—a drink, a snack, a trip to the bathroom, the TV remote, the heat on, the heat off, etc. Seriously, I wouldn't trade anything for having him home, and he wouldn't trade anything for sleeping in his own bed.

So we were on to the next level. As we left Shepherd Center, Bruce proudly wore the marathon medal that had hung at the foot of his bed for so long—waiting for this moment.

Bringing him home from the hospital was scary—for both of us. We had been in the comfort and care of people who knew what to do. Now it was only Bruce and me at home with Princess. Some adaptations to the house had to be made. Bruce was using a wheelchair and a walker a little bit. Our living and sleeping areas were on the same floor, so that made things easier. Our future son-in-law and his stepfather installed some handrails on our front porch steps, which proved to be invaluable. A bench and hand-held shower nozzle were installed, and gratefully, that was about all we had to do besides slowing down our pace of living. I had learned so much about caring for Bruce at Shepherd Center, but now was the time I had to do it all on my own—with God's help.

The day before my birthday was his homecoming day—the greatest gift ever. His dad and sister came and cooked steaks with all the trimmings for dinner—while Rachel and I went to Spa Sydell for two hours of facials and massages—a gift from Bruce as a thank you for the past eleven weeks. I felt guilty *at first* for leaving him with his steak dinner, but I got over it quickly after the first few seconds of the massage. I didn't know I had so many knotted up muscles, but the massage therapist found every one.

On Sunday, Bruce slept until 9:30 a.m.—a first in three months since there's not much chance for that in a hospital. The next Sunday was Easter, so we went to church with Rachel by our side. Bruce was thrilled to be dressed as a "real person." The fact he was in a wheelchair didn't matter; he was glad to be anywhere outside the hospital. Rachel had been such a strong gal through all of this, but as she sat next to her dad and thought over the past three months, her tears began to flow uncontrollably. What better place to "let go" than at church where God surrounded her with His love.

Our church was very faithful and constant in prayer during the previous three months. At the end of the service, the pastor said, "We've been praying for Bruce Allen since January first, and he's here this morning!" Bruce stood, with Rachel's help, and the congregation gave him a long standing ovation. What a blessing it was for Bruce to experience their support first hand, and for the congregation to actually see the answer to their prayers. They have continued to support us in many ways, and we are grateful beyond words for such a caring church. To top off Easter Sunday, Bruce's family brought food, and we shared a joyous lunch together at home.

Our neighbors knew nothing of our journey since I was never home to tell them. When they saw us taking a stroll outside with the walker, they came out, asked a million questions, and then brought us some meals for our time of adjustment at home. We live in a very special neighborhood with very special friends.

We headed to Shepherd Pathways, the outpatient rehab center, with great anticipation. The therapists challenged him even more to push toward the next level of recovery and worked on his occupational needs. I'm glad they encouraged him to work on his computer skills, which were so important to him in his work, but it was OK with me if working with the Blackberry was put off until the very end. I had gotten used to the silence and peace without its constant ringing.

Each weekday morning, the Shepherd Center van met us fifteen minutes from our house at 7:30 a.m., to take Bruce and some other outpatients to Pathways. Each afternoon, the van brought him back so I could pick him up. I didn't know how dark it could be at 6:30 a.m., but we adjusted to the new schedule by going to bed at 8 p.m. each evening. The use of the van shuttle saved us a lot of money and time on the road.

Bruce showed great advancement in therapy. His right side was still weak, so that was a main focus at Pathways. He was still having some aphasia and couldn't always find the right words to say. Now *that* was tough for a preacher. However, the therapist assured us his speech would improve—with prayer and in God's timing.

BRUCE'S THOUGHTS

While at Shepherd Center as an inpatient, I became friends with some wonderful and interesting people. Patients of all ages had had motorcycle wrecks, car wrecks, falls, strokes, and tumors. I'm still in touch with many of them by phone and email today. There is a strong connection between brain injury survivors because they know they have friends who understand what they are going through.

Finally the day came to go home. This is a big day in anyone's therapy. I wanted to go home. I was ready to see Princess and my friends. However, I was apprehensive about the days that were ahead. For instance, I had to get out of a wheelchair, onto the sliding board, and into the seat of our car. This was not as easy as you might think, but I was ready to risk it to go home.

I felt so unnatural riding in a car after being in the hospital for six weeks. It seemed like every car was coming directly at me. Laura was driving entirely too fast. On the trip home, I'm sure I told her at least ten times, "Look out—you are going to hit that car!" After living life at two miles per hour, I felt like I was traveling on the Atlanta Speedway at break-neck speeds.

After a short drive which seemed like a very long drive to me, I was back home for the first time in ten weeks. This was an exciting moment. I remember going into the house and seeing all the colors, decorations, flowers, and plants. Everything seemed full of life—vibrant and exciting. Overwhelmed, I cried as I walked into the house. It felt so good to be home. Yet it felt scary as well.

I enjoyed a delicious home-cooked meal that evening. To be surrounded at home by my family, who had been so supportive during this journey, was also overwhelming. I had always been fairly strong and capable, and now it seemed like I was a retired, old man. I wondered if I would ever get back to normal strength or even a faint facsimile of what I had been before. These sorts of thoughts play on the mind and cause worry and anxiety.

My exhortation to a brain injury survivor would be to take one day at a time. Don't get too far ahead of yourself. Enjoy the moment, and enjoy it for what it is. Remember: it is what it is. It was wonderful to sleep in my own bed again. A hospital bed can *never* feel like your own bed. Laura installed a railing for the side of the bed that slipped under the mattress for stability. It made me feel secure, and I could grab on if I needed it. I was so grateful that I didn't have to be turned every two hours during the night anymore.

Our first Sunday back at church was indescribable. Laura and Rachel pushed my wheelchair to the end of the pew where they sat. I enjoyed the singing, praise, and worship. I really enjoyed being with people who had prayed so much for me while I was in the hospital. Pastor Mark Walker recognized that I was there. It was a joyous moment for me as the whole congregation stood and applauded God for the miracle that was before their eyes. It was like a homecoming, and was a great part of my therapy.

To see how God had worked and provided in ways we didn't even realize we needed was awesome. After a severe brain injury, when life turned upside-down, I really appreciated life and realized that we don't have as much control over life as we think we do. At the end of the day, life comes down to faith and trust in God—for everything.

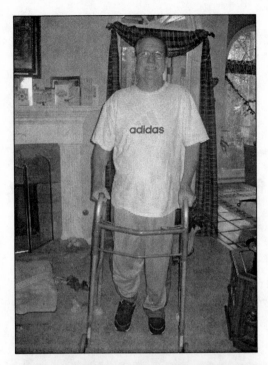

Home at Last!

Chapter 17

The Next Twenty Weeks

LAURA'S THOUGHTS

UPDATE
Pathways, March 25, 2008

Bruce has had a full week at Pathways. The therapists are really working him to strengthen his arm and leg—and they are making progress. His speech is almost 100% back. He doesn't fish for words like he used to, and his eyes are always improving ever so slightly. In June we'll go to a neuro-ophthalmologist to have his eyes checked and glasses fitted. The friends he met at Shepherd Center are now at Pathways with him, so they have lunch together each day and encourage one another.

The therapists are taking away his wheelchair next week, and he will depend totally on the walker. It is still a waiting game as the swelling in the brain continues to decrease. It may take another six months to a year for the swelling to completely go down. Perseverance and determination are Bruce's two strengths, along with his faith.

Bruce's progress was amazing. The therapists took away his wheelchair and walked him completely with only his walker and ankle boot. His floppy foot was still not showing any response, so he was sent to a specialist to see why the nerve signals in the brain were not reaching the ankle. He also tried a four-footed cane which would be his next mode of travel. He was still a bit unstable when he walked, but he was growing stronger each day.

The therapists asked him to type some dictated words on the computer. His mind totally blocked out the keyboard (some days I wish *I* could block it out), and his right hand would not type. He realized he was going to have to learn this skill again. We eventually bought "Naturally Speaking," a computer program that records his voice through a microphone and types his words on the computer. It was exactly what he needed, and has been invaluable in writing this book.

At this point, his speech was about 98% back. No longer did he stumble over words or struggle to find the right ones. That was a real relief to this preacher. I was glad he remembered how to speak English (since he had forgotten how to type). If he had awakened from surgery speaking Japanese, we would have been in a real pickle. That *has* happened to some people. One of our friends in our brain injury support group awoke from surgery speaking English with a British accent. She's from Alabama. *That* was a shock to her family. Even now, three years after her injury, she speaks with a beautiful British accent.

At home in his own bed (and sleeping with his wife), Bruce didn't experience any pain whatsoever. That was such a real and constant problem in the hospital at first. I think Pathways was working him so hard that he didn't have time to think about the pain.

We played many games of Uno to work on his numbers. A trip to Great Clips shaped up his Marine haircut. He was most proud when he was able to write his signature with his right hand. He met each challenge head-on, and his labors were being rewarded.

Bruce was one of the first of his new Shepherd friends to migrate to Pathways. As the others arrived one by one, the therapists were amazed at how the incoming patients all knew him and lit up when they saw him. Bruce said these were his "flock."

We both have met people and done things that we would never have done if we had stayed in our comfort zone. Even in difficult times, the journey has been counted all joy when walking it with the Lord leading the way.

BRUCE'S THOUGHTS

After a much too brief weekend at home, Laura loaded me up in the Blazer, wheelchair and all, and took me to Cumberland Mall to meet my new rehab buddies. The Shepherd Center van was there to pick us up every weekday for the next twenty weeks. She simply dropped me off, and Greg, the driver, stopped for other patients along the way as we headed toward Pathways.

Those rides were so enjoyable. Greg was a jovial, affable black man who loved people and life. He had a real joy and happiness about him. He used the wheelchair lift to pick me up and get me into the van. Then he would lock me down so that I wouldn't roll around.

A kind and thoughtful man, Greg stopped at McDonald's on some days to get coffee and sausage biscuits for the five or six of us. His acts of kindness made us feel like we were back in the real world. After all, what's more "real world" than McDonald's? We solved all of the problems of the world—and baseball—on those rides. At the time, I didn't realize how much more rehab I needed. I thought I could do rehab at home myself. What a mistake that would have been.

After being unloaded from the van, I rolled into the room at Pathways and was thrilled to see some of my old buddies from Shepherd Center sitting there. "Hey, Darrel! Andy! Courtney!" We were like a bunch of eight-year-olds in a candy store. I still call them on a regular basis, and they call me. Having these friends has been a huge part of my therapy. I have come to appreciate everything in life much more—my wife, family, people, food, things, and places.

Each morning at Pathways began with an opening session where all of the patients gathered before going to their individual therapists. Thomas, a tall black man who could really play the keyboard and sing, led us in music therapy, which helped us rebuild our word bank. He also read the newspaper to us to keep us up-to- date on current events. He was like our cheerleader, helping to start the day with the right attitude.

We then headed off to a variety of therapies. We experienced physical therapy as well as speech, occupational, exercise, balance, and recreational therapies. The rooms were filled with machines to develop the various therapies. I even had dance therapy—for a Baptist preacher, that was a real trip. I wasn't coordinated enough to dance before my surgery, much less after. We also played games to get to know others and to develop our communication skills. I loved to move pieces around the game board and compete with the patients. It was fun, as well as challenging. We brought our own lunches, and all forty of us ate outside if it were nice, or inside where we could also play foosball and pool. Even during lunch time, we were experiencing rehab.

Each therapist had her own specialty. They were all young and really cute. Maybe that was why we looked forward to therapy each day. Suzanne, my psychologist, would ask how things were going. She always encouraged me to keep moving forward, and I felt safe as I shared my inner feelings with her. Kathryn, my physical therapist, helped me with my balance and walking. She was engaged. I offered to perform her wedding for free, but she didn't take me up on it. Lindsey, my speech therapist, challenged me at every level to keep speaking in order to get back to where I was. She knew that I'd been a minister who spoke extemporaneously without thinking about what I would say next. Now I was struggling with each word and an inability to even remember words. She was very patient and kind. Sherry, my occupational therapist, worked with my illegible handwriting and tried to make my right arm more useable. She was gentle, but she kept me on track if I tended to chase rabbits.

One of my favorite verses in the Bible says, "Those who trust in the Lord will find new strength. They will soar high on wings like eagles" (Isaiah 40:31). When God tells us to trust Him, He doesn't mean to stop and do nothing! We must do the things the therapists tell us to do. They are not going to ask us to do things we are not able to do. I may think I'm not able, but the therapists know I *am* able.

Besides renewing friendships from Shepherd Center, I made many new friends at Pathways. I was very outgoing before my injury, but afterward, I was even more so. As I met people, they would automatically tell me their problems. (Maybe they could "tell" I was a minister. Laura said I was a people magnet.)

Some people's deficits are more obvious than others, which is a problem for a brain injured person. A survivor might appear to have no deficits, but after talking with him, some issues might be obvious—or the issues might not be obvious at all. Deficits can be external, like the inability to walk, or internal, like aphasia or short-term memory problems.

My right arm was gradually gaining some function, so the time had come to graduate from Velcro tennis shoes to shoes with laces. Rachel showed me how to tie my shoes. I practiced and practiced to achieve this lost ability. Later, as I watched the movie, *Regarding Henry*, starring Harrison Ford, that same scene played out. Henry had suffered a TBI and was relearning all of his everyday skills. His ten-year-old daughter was showing him how to tie his shoes. He looked at her quizzically and asked, "Where did you learn to do that?" When she responded, "You taught me, Daddy," I cried.

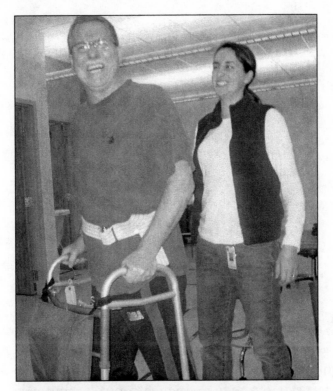

Rehab is hard work.

Chapter 18

Right Side Neglect

LAURA'S THOUGHTS

Many people who experience aphasia also have weakness or paralysis in their right leg and right arm. Aphasia *and* right side neglect are usually acquired due to the damage on the left side of the brain, which controls movements on the right side of the body.

Right side neglect is one of the brain's little tricks. The brain does not acknowledge that the right side exists. Bruce continued to wear the foot brace in his shoe and to sleep with the bi-valve to hopefully train his brain to hold up that foot. However, his right arm had a mind of its own. As we watched TV, Bruce's right hand would be up in the air. I'd ask, "Are you voting?" And he'd say, "Oh, I didn't know where my hand was." This occurred frequently, and still does today. The brain forgets that the right side exists, so the right side has its own movements at odd times—rising up, getting caught in the car seatbelt without Bruce's awareness, and unconsciously tipping a drink until it spills.

BRUCE'S THOUGHTS

The right side of the brain controls the left side of the body, and vice versa. It is amazing to see how the brain functions—or doesn't function—with a brain injury. Our daughter, Rachel, who is left-handed, is quick to tell me that she is the only one who is in her right mind since she's left-handed. I have what is called right side neglect. I really can't tell where my right side is in relationship to the rest of my body. When I reach for something in a cabinet, my right hand will go too far right and miss the object completely. My depth perception is way off.

A quick way to determine how your brain works is to close your eyes and touch the tip of your nose with your left hand. Then close your eyes and touch the tip of your nose with your right hand. In my case, my right hand is always about one foot past my face. This exercise simply points out that my perception is not what I think it is. I'm about half of a bubble off. Particularly when I hug someone, I have to be careful where my right hand is. When I hug a woman, if I'm not careful, I'll reach around and place my right hand on her breast instead of her arm. I must be very careful when I hug women at church—or anywhere else. Of course, some guys think this is a great excuse, but my right hand's placement is really directly related to my depth perception. Like the famous philosopher, Forrest Gump states, "That's all I have to say about that."

I never know exactly where my arm is in space. When I first started going to rehab at Pathways, I noticed that my right arm was raised up high, but I didn't realize it. We put a two-pound weight on my right hand, but the hand still went up. I also experienced a floppy foot on my right side. I couldn't lift up my foot enough to walk properly, so it dragged as I tried to make it work right. Even today before I stand, I have to look at my feet to be sure my right leg is underneath me. Otherwise, if I stand up in a hurry, I'll fall back into the chair. People with brain injuries have to be more careful. Movements are more calculated.

My driving is a little slower, because I'm more cautious. I do have a note in my car from Dr. Kaelin stating that I have some issues with my right side which affect my walking. If I were stopped by a policeman and asked to walk a straight line, I wouldn't be able to do it, no matter how hard I'd try. That's when I would whip out my trusty note to verify I'm not three sheets in the wind.

As I was learning to drive again, I could not press the accelerator with the right foot and also brake with my right foot. My Shepherd Center driving instructor told me to use the right foot for the accelerator and the left for the brake, but there are many other adaptive ways to get back to driving again. If driving is a possibility for you as a brain injury survivor, I encourage you to try because getting out and going where I want enables me to have some sense of freedom.

Chapter 19

More Doctors— and Graduation

LAURA'S THOUGHTS

UPDATE
Pathways, April 22, 2008

We visited a neuro-ophthalmologist (with her own helicopter on the roof of the office for emergency calls). She did a full two-hour exam and checked <u>every</u> inch of Bruce's eyesight. His eyes had not changed much from where they were before this part of the journey began. The change was the same as for any fifty-three-year-old man who merely grew a year older. Since he lost most of his eyesight due to the second brain surgery and couldn't see for a month, this is a miracle. We were led to believe there might be some permanent damage. The only damage he has is due to getting older. Again, God has shown He is the Great Healer.

Bruce has graduated from the walker to a cane and is doing very well with it. He arises in the morning, showers, dresses himself, and comes to breakfast all on his own. One month ago, none of that was possible. I continue to be amazed at how far he has come in three and a half months.

Today we met with the neurosurgeon who performed his surgery. He said Bruce was looking good and doing very well in -his recovery. Bruce has a three-inch by four-inch hole in his skull that was left open to accommodate the swelling of the brain. On June 6, Dr. Benedict will do the surgery to insert a plastic plate. He said it will be custom-made to fit Bruce's skull opening exactly. He will set it in place with a few screws to secure it, and then Bruce will stay in the hospital two to three days for observation. If I ever say he has a few loose screws in his head, I might be right!

A CT scan and an MRI were done in preparation for the surgery. The doctors said they didn't see anything—boy, did I have a good time with that comment.

Tomorrow Bruce will swim at rehab. He is really enjoying his time at Pathways too much. On May 16, his day program will change to two to three afternoons per week.

We have been told it will be six months to a year to reach full recovery. Please keep praying as the advancements slow down.

God is so faithful—in all things. He may not give us what we want when we want it, but he gives us what we need when we need it. We saw so many miracles through Shepherd Center over those four months:

- Bruce progressed from the bed to a wheelchair to a walker to a four-footed cane to a regular cane.

- His eyesight returned to where it was before the surgery.

- His memory was excellent—and really was never affected.

- The therapists worked with his handwriting on his weaker right side.

- His right leg was getting stronger through the exercises.569

- His speaking—well, he never had been at a loss for words, had he?

What God was still working on:
- Bruce's typing skills were still being revived.

- His walking was improving little by little—the cane would be gone someday.

What I was working on:

- Teaching him to stop being a front seat driver!

- Breaking him of his ice cream stop every afternoon on the way home from Pathways!

- Re-establishing his home chores. He was great at emptying the dishwasher and doing the dishes (boy, had I missed that since January), and we worked in the yard as he shaped the pine straw beds and watered the newly planted flowers. If I could only get him to do laundry, I would have a major victory—but that never will happen.

Proverbs 3:5–6 has been and is our mainstay: " Trust in the Lord with all your heart; do not depend on your own understanding. Seek His will in all you do, and He will show you which path to take." At times we may start to ask "What if...," but trusting in the Lord gave us a peace that passes all understanding when we know He is in control of everything. Leaning on our own understanding only gets us in trouble. Bruce has never asked, "Why did this happen to me?" Instead, he asks, "How does God want to use this experience for His Glory?"

BRUCE'S THOUGHTS

My rehab schedule at Pathways changed to three afternoons a week. Laura drove me to Pathways and worked there on her computer for three hours while I was in therapy. The stop for ice cream on the way home was a small pleasure we did not need, but we felt we deserved. We took a week or two off from therapy for vacations to see family. It was so good to have a break from rehab.

After twenty weeks at Pathways, my graduation day finally arrived. It was a joyous day in many ways. However, it was also a sad day. Why? Because after being in therapy for twenty weeks and having spent many hours each day with these therapists, I became very attached to them. They were a part of my life, and to imagine going on without them seemed a bit scary. I was ready to start living life in the real world, but I didn't want to lose the new friendships I had made. I guess that is part of growth, development, and moving on. It was time to cut the apron strings and fly on my own.

For graduation from Pathways, I had to do a project on the computer. I was to use a PowerPoint presentation to explain what it was like to have a brain injury. It was a teaching and talking explanation with a slideshow. Through this project, the therapists were giving me a platform to use some of my teaching skills again and to build my confidence. I put a lot of thought into this project which literally made my brain hurt. Who would think giving a talk to five of my favorite therapists could be so terrifying? I nervously presented my slides, talked fast, and got to the end as quickly as I could. They applauded widely, so I guess it went well. I was just relieved to be finished. After the presentation, my therapists put a graduation hat on me and instructed me to move the tassel from one side to the other. It was truly graduation day as I moved from organized rehab into the rehab center of life. What an experience that proved to be!

Pathways Graduation

Chapter 20

The Final Surgery
and Onward!

LAURA'S THOUGHTS

UPDATE
Kennestone Hospital, May 29, 2008

Surgery day! It went perfectly. Dr. Benedict put the three-inch by four-inch plastic
plate in Bruce's head to cover the hole in his skull and secured it with titanium
micro-screws. Bruce was in the hospital for three days in the same neuro-ICU
where this journey had started. It was like a big reunion. On Sunday, we were off
to First Baptist Church, Centerville, Georgia, to thank the people there for their
prayers and love. Bruce pastored in this community for nine years, and we wanted
to personally thank the prayer warriors for their faithfulness. Three days later, we
left on a much-needed vacation to Illinois to see my family and relax—away from
rehab, my work, home upkeep, and paying bills. Yes, Princess went with us.

The entire process since January 1 was amazing—very
exhausting, but amazing and miraculous. Sharing the
victories with my family in Illinois was wonderful. My ninety-
one-year-old mother was thrilled to see his progress. "I'm glad
you are going to be around to do my funeral," she said, which
he did six months later. It was a beautiful service.

We decided to be daring when, with Rachel, we flew to San Francisco to spend a few days with our son and his fiancée. That was a trial run to see what "real life" was going to be. I would never have tried this with Bruce alone. Having Rachel with us, our resident ABI nurse/daughter, was a tremendous blessing. I had no concerns with her along. She was and is still a wonder with her dad. In San Francisco, we took a slower pace than usual—resting, sleeping, and seeing the sights. It was great to see Jason and Joanna again, and to enjoy doing something different than rehab with them. However, when we returned home, Bruce crashed on the couch for four days to recuperate.

The third step of the journey was now beginning. The initial surgery and five weeks in neuro-ICU, five weeks as an inpatient at Shepherd Center, and then twenty weeks at Pathways were all in preparation for living life as a brain injury survivor in the real world. We had finally arrived. And it was scary.

Bruce frequently said, "This has been the best year of my life." He enjoyed reflecting on what life is all about, what God's purpose is for his life, and spending more time with family. It was not necessarily the best year of *my* life, but it was truly a spiritually growing experience that I cherish more with each passing day.

Pathways gave Bruce a totally new group to relate to. He had always been a people person, but since brain surgery, the right hemisphere of his brain took the lead. He was more outgoing than before, never meeting a stranger, and had a kind, encouraging word for everyone he talked with. He developed a list of friends at Shepherd Center and Pathways with whom he now stays in regular contact by phone. He is such an encouragement to them, and, in turn, they encourage him.

The left hemisphere of the brain is the organized, number-crunching part of the brain. The abscesses were in Bruce's left hemisphere. The numbers were gradually coming back, so Bruce could do some addition. In March, 2+2 was a tough one for him. He slowly progressed to adding two and three-digit numbers.

Bruce's right side function was still only about 60% of the strength that he had before, but as he worked out at the gym, that improved as well. However, he still needed his leg brace to hold his right foot in walking position.

At his six-month checkup at Shepherd Center, Bruce received a good report. He still had some improvement to gain, but the doctor said that would happen during the next six months or so. February 2009 was projected for the possibility of Bruce taking his driver's test. He'd been practicing in the church parking lot and doing very well (as long as there were no other cars around). His peripheral vision still had some difficulty on both sides, but a lot could happen before February.

In September, after completing his rehab at Pathways, Bruce performed a wedding ceremony for some close family friends from Centerville. The wedding was held in Greensboro, Georgia, at a gorgeous old antebellum home with an outdoor chapel and reception area. Bruce did great at the wedding. Doing something like that for the first time after brain surgery can be a little nerve-wracking, but he came through beautifully! It was good practice for performing Jason and Joanna's wedding the following May in Santa Barbara, California.

Some friends took him to lunch during the week while I was at work. He certainly enjoyed the fellowship and change of scenery. Another dear friend took him to Turner Field to see the Atlanta Braves play—and miraculously win. What a day that was for him. Slowly he was getting back to "normal."

BRUCE'S THOUGHTS

I had one final surgery during which Dr. Benedict replaced the piece of my skull that was taken out during the original surgery. That made three brain surgeries. I hoped he was planning to leave something in there. Since the skull was contaminated with a strep infection, Dr. Benedict put a plastic piece custom-made to fit the hole in my head. He tightened it down with titanium screws and told Laura that she could hit me in the head with a frying pan and it wouldn't crack. That's a dangerous thing to tell a wife! The titanium screws would not set off the alarms at the airport, so I was ready to fly. Often the original piece of skull is put back in the hole; the piece is put in the person's abdomen (because the body won't reject it later) or in a freezer for six months until it is ready to be put back in during surgery. That's what happened to my friend, a fireman who fell off a fire truck. He looked like his head had been hit with a bowling ball. However, after the swelling of the brain went down, his doctors pulled the skull piece out of the freezer and put it back in his head. My friend looked like he did before the accident.

Remember—sleep is important because the brain heals during sleep. I definitely am more tired than I used to be. I sleep nine or ten hours a night and still need a nap in the afternoon. However, I cannot sleep all day and then expect big accomplishments in therapy. I've discovered that I can do maybe two major things in a day. However, if I overdo and try to cram three activities into the day, I end up paying the price of exhaustion the next day. I've learned to pace myself.

Brain injuries can change a person's personality and views. I was very much of a right-wing person politically, theologically, and spiritually. Everything I did or thought was to the extreme right. After my surgery, I noticed that my views moved toward the middle. For instance, before my surgery, I enjoyed listening to Sean Hannity on Fox News. I would also listen to Neal Boortz and Rush Limbaugh. However, my brain injury caused me to neglect my right-winged views. Talk about right-side neglect! This doesn't mean that I don't believe anything, but rather I am a more in the middle in my thinking. I used to be all black and white in my views, but now I am open to shades of gray. I've realized that things can't always be divided into black or white. I'm more open to other views and situations in life, in general,

I suppose. I'm much more accepting and happy. I am at peace with myself and who I am—and with who other people are.

Rachel and Laura say I used to be very driven. Now I am much more relaxed and happy-go-lucky. Whatever the weather is, I'm happy with it. A brain injury does not ever leave you exactly the same as before, but it can change you for the better!

My awareness of God has also changed. I know that there is part of the brain that is called the God center. Tests have shown that when people are in prayer or meditation, this part of the brain is activated. The God center of my brain seems to be activated all the time now. There is not one moment when I do not sense God's presence with me. When I was a pastor, there would be moments of despair and times of joy. However, now the God part of my brain seems to be overstimulated to the point that I'm constantly aware of the fact that in God I move and live and have my being. In fact, besides all the damage that was done by my brain injury, one thing that was not affected was my memory for Scripture. All the verses that I had memorized as a college student and as a seminary student are still very much a part of me. I can remember the exact verses and their locations in the Bible.

God has definitely been with Laura and me throughout this entire experience. We could not have survived it without Him, family, and each other.

> For I have chosen you and will not throw you away.
> Don't be afraid, for I am with you.
> Don't be discouraged, for I am your God.
> I will strengthen you and help you.
> I will hold you up with my victorious right hand.
> Isaiah 41:9b–10

Chapter 21

The New Normal

LAURA'S THOUGHTS

UPDATE
October 19, 2008

We are so very grateful for the way God has met every need—physically, emotionally, and spiritually. Since September 1, through Shepherd Center's Bridge Program, Bruce has continued to work with a therapist two to three times a week. We have taken some trips. Last week, we spent a few days in Hiawassee, Georgia, to enjoy the leaves and some R & R—for Laura! With the economy slow down, Social Security Disability has been another one of God's special ways of providing. We stand amazed each day at His faithfulness and the inner peace that He gives.

I'll sound the warning when Bruce takes to the road driving again.

When I had asked Dr. Benedict after Bruce's initial surgery, "How long will it take until he is back to normal?" his very wise response was, "It will take as long as it takes." Dr. Benedict didn't comment on whether or not "normal" was attainable. "Normal" is definitely in the eyes of the beholder. I think we all gauge what is normal by comparing people to ourselves. Of course, we each think we are the normal one, and others have their little quirks that give them different shades of being normal.

After a brain injury, a person can have difficulty deciding what is normal. The brain has been tumbled around, and depending on the severity of that tumble, it may never return to how it was before. However, who said Bruce was normal before? Our brain injury survivor friends call life after their injuries the "new normal." Every aspect of life is changed and altered. When the person can accept these changes and make use of adaptations where needed, he will find he can enjoy life—perhaps even more than before—in his form of the "new normal."

Bruce was always very active, high energy, busy, on the move, and on top of things. Now he needs ten to twelve hours of sleep a day, along with a nap in the afternoon. His body and brain don't have the stamina they once had. However, when he is alert, he is more calm, patient, and ready to laugh at himself when he says the wrong word or does the unexpected. With a brain injury, we have to adapt to expecting the unexpected. Bruce may find himself putting a tube of cortisone on his toothbrush. He may try to brush his hair with his toothbrush. As he cuts meat with a knife, he may try to use the dull side of the blade instead of the sharp edge. He'll put the napkins in the refrigerator and the milk on the cabinet. His brain is trying to make new pathways by firing the neurons in the right direction, but it doesn't always happen. Since this would be very frustrating to most of us, a sense of humor is the number one prerequisite to being a brain injury survivor. When Bruce does something that is definitely out of the normal (there's that word), we have a good laugh and think about how really amazing the brain is.

We learned to adapt to the new normal. In our case, we have found we actually like the new normal better than the old normal. We function at a slower, more relaxed pace. I have learned to allow more time to get ready and be on time. We had to take "the rush" out of everyday living—and I think we'll live longer for it. Bruce was always running in high gear, as was I, but that changed in January 2008.

Bruce's executive functions returned with some deficits, and we have found his organizational and planning skills are lacking. He has learned to make notes and reminders for everything. He cannot operate a computer, but the Blackberry is his best pal. He puts appointments on his calendar, and an alarm goes off to remind him that he is to be somewhere soon—he is using technology to adapt to his new normal.

As he continued to improve in his walking and balance issues, Bruce liked using his Blackberry as a phone, but he missed having access to email. Again, the lack of skills on the computer almost stopped him dead in his tracks. Once again, the Blackberry brought him into the world of instant communication. When he realized that he can operate the Blackberry keyboard with his two thumbs, we activated the email function. Now he can email his friends with brief thoughts when he wants to. This is a long way from lying in the hospital bed saying, "I want…" and feeling trapped in his body.

One area that has not been mentioned is the financial strain inherent with the loss of the main bread winner's monthly check. When Bruce decided to branch out on his own with Mark Brooks, who formed The Charis Group, a capital stewardship campaign company, we didn't have a big corporation to lean on for health benefits. We were self-employed with no insurance of any kind. I immediately started looking for a job that would provide insurance for our family. Rachel was in nursing school, and I was familiar with her program of study. I looked on Kennesaw State University's School of Nursing website and was surprised to see a job posting that sounded like it was written specifically for me. Honestly, why was I surprised? God knew our need—and knew what was coming down the road—so He provided the perfect career with great benefits. However, we didn't even think about long-term disability insurance for Bruce. After all, he was only fifty-two years old at the time.

As the brain storm descended upon us a year later, the insurance covered everything except $200. God miraculously provided for our need before we even knew we were going to have it. Bruce had some work commissions and payments that he hadn't received yet when the storm began to swirl, and that income sustained us, along with my salary, through those first six months. Shepherd Center's assistance with the application for Social Security Disability was another direction from God. The month the funds from The Charis Group ran out was the same month the Social Security Disability check started coming in. Some things are just too perfectly engineered to be coincidental. We certainly have had to tighten up a lot in our budget to keep the bills paid. If you need help in your situation, many foundations and organizations exist to help you through these muddy waters of financial strain. Some are listed in the Resources section at the end of this book. Don't be afraid to ask them for help. This is why they exist.

Our daughter, Rachel, made the observation that her dad had changed a lot in the way he approached life. Losing the busy, overly active guy wasn't so bad when we now had someone who was more compassionate, outgoing, and able to see more of the funny side of life. She said, "I like Dad better now than before. We lost Mr. Organization, but we got to keep the fun side of Dad." The new normal is good!

BRUCE'S THOUGHTS

Life is one giant rehabilitation lab. Going to the grocery store is rehab. Finding items on the shelf is rehab. Paying for your purchases is rehab. (Since counting out the money is impossible for me, I have to trust the clerk when I hand over money and expect change in return). Working out at the gym is rehab.

A brain injury can cause you to do strange things. When I start to brush my hair, I always face the brush wrong side up away from my hair. As I put toothpaste on my toothbrush, the toothbrush is often upside down. I have learned to live with these peculiarities. A sense of humor is invaluable.

Keeping the body temperature regulated can often be a challenge for the brain. During the daytime, my right side can feel cool. However, when I go to bed at night, my right side becomes very hot, and I kick the covers off. In an hour or two, my body temperature returns to normal. Life is never boring with a brain injury.

Being in large crowds still bothers me. I cannot be in a large room with a lot of people without feeling that everything is spinning. When we go to the mall, the airport, or even at church, I follow Laura as if she is running interference for me on a football field. I feel like all of these people are rushing right at me. I become dizzy and disoriented.

As I finished at Pathways, I didn't want to be completely on my own. Laura learned that Shepherd Center sponsored the Bridge Program, which is designed to help a recently released patient to acclimate to his new life and everyday events at home. Bernie Marcus, co-founder of Home Depot, sponsors and supports this program as well as a unit at Shepherd Center dedicated to brain injured soldiers returning from Iraq and Afghanistan. One of the things I wanted to do before I die was to meet Bernie Marcus. That wish was fulfilled recently, and I have a picture to prove it. I was able to shake his hand and say, "Thank you, thank you so much for everything you've done for me and for all those servicemen."

The Bridge Program was very good for me. I was taught how to do basic things at home. The therapist came to our house and helped me put together a menu and shopping list. We went to the store and purchased the items. She then helped me cook the meal. Opening a can of soup, finding the right pot and putting it on the stove to heat may seem like basic movements, but for me, the entire process was very stressful.

My Bridge Program therapist was very competent and instilled confidence in me. She asked what kinds of things I liked to do. Yard work was a favorite that I had really missed over the past eight months. We went to Pike's Nursery, bought some flowers, and planted them in the front yard. It was so beautiful! I had such a feeling of accomplishment. Again, life itself is a giant rehab center.

Shepherd Center also sponsored a day at Lake Allatoona north of Atlanta, Georgia, for those who had graduated from the program. This fun day was another part of the Bridge Program. The therapists brought canoes, paddle boats, jet skis, a pontoon, and a big picnic. It was marvelous! I had not been on the lake since I went to the hospital in January. Getting out on the water on the jet ski was awesome. It was like new-found freedom all over again. I was so thrilled that I could swim. I had been swimming in the Shepherd Center pool, but nothing is like the lake and sunshine.

During Lake Allatoona Day, Scott McEvoy, one of my brain injury friends and a former commercial airline pilot, and I decided that we would go out in a canoe. After the therapists helped us put on our lifejackets, we were on our way. We walked to the edge of the water and stepped in the canoe. As we tried to push off, we thought it would be easy. However, as we lunged to move the canoe into the water, we tipped to the right and fell over on our sides. We laid there in the sand, laughing and trying to figure out how to get out. The therapists helped us get out into the water, and we finally had fun canoeing. Again, things take a little more time and care after a brain injury.

Before my surgery, I was a good slalom water skier and a hotdog snow skier. Shepherd Center sponsored an adaptive skiing clinic at the lake that fulfilled one of my dreams. I thought I'd never be able to ski again due to my right side neglect. However, adaptive skiing shattered that myth. An adaptive ski has a seat made of net situated on a wide, single ski. The brain injury survivor sits in the seat, and the ski rope is knotted and slipped in a slot on the front of the ski. As the boat pulls the ski up out of the water, the skier sits in the seat and can reach down and pick up the rope handle to hold on if he chooses to. It is like water skiing, only sitting down. I never thought I would ever ski again, and here I was! Adaptive snow skiing is on the schedule for next year.

Lake Allatoona Day

Sit Skiing

Chapter 22

Life: The Ultimate Therapy Lab

LAURA'S THOUGHTS

UPDATE
March 1, 2009

Bruce finally got the neuro-psych test results from his neuro-psychologist, Dr. Rob Godsall. The test was four hours long, and wore Bruce out. He said it involved too much thinking for a guy who has had brain surgery! The doctors' responses were, "Your recovery is truly a miracle." We already knew that, didn't we?

Bruce took a four-hour driving evaluation to see if he could get his driver's license. Driving involves coordinating what he sees with the control of the steering wheel and the pedal or brake when he needs to make a split-second decision. He passed. So beware world—Bruce is behind the wheel! This opened a whole new world of independence for him.

Dr. Kaelin said Bruce's problem with the numbers is "attentional." Bruce can add the numbers, but as he tries to do that, the brain stops paying attention for a moment, so he doesn't give the right addition number. The doctor said to continue to challenge Bruce's brain with many varieties of activities, and the attention when doing details like spelling or math will strengthen. The brain is truly an amazing organ. Just when I think he has forgotten how to add numbers, we're told that he knows how, but the brain takes a break while doing that detailed activity.

Things are moving forward. Bruce continues to improve (getting rid of the foot brace is a huge step forward), and God is so good.

Everything Bruce does is therapy—getting dressed, feeding himself, shopping at the grocery store, and punching the numbers into the phone, which is a *real* challenge to a guy who has problems working with numbers. Every move he takes is practice for the next level. His positive outlook toward the challenges continues to amaze me. It's like he is a child discovering something new in life every day with wonder and excitement. "Never give up" is his motto.

Now what? Formal therapy sessions were over, and Bruce had a lot of time of his hands. So he decided to put it to good use. His eyes were not functioning well enough to read at first, so he checked out books on discs from the library. He loved to "read" books of all types. The news on CNN was a mainstay. He had a lot to catch up on.

Bruce loves to be with people—particularly others who have also experienced brain injuries to learn adapting tools from them. A brain injury support group meets at Kennestone Hospital once a month, so we are faithful attenders. About forty-five brain injury survivors meet together, learn, share, have a good time, and help each other learn new skills. The brain injury group also has fun socially. They go bowling, boat riding on a pontoon belonging to one of the members of the group, have coffee during the week besides Fridays, and help each other with their own specific situations.

Bruce started having coffee with one or two people from the support group on Fridays, then three or four, then ten, twenty. Now they meet for breakfast at the Whistlestop Café every Friday at 10 a.m., and they have a ball together. There are no inhibitions, and no subjects are off limits. It's a time for friends to become better friends. When Leah, a beautiful young stroke survivor, noticed that three people were having difficulties reading the menu, she created a little picture book for each of them so they could show the waitress what they would like to order. She saw a need and acted on it to help her new friends. When people come to the Kennestone group, they are automatically invited to the breakfast. Soon the group will have to move to a larger restaurant.

Once a week Bruce volunteers at MUST Ministries, which is a large operation that gives clothes, food, bread, medical treatment, etc., to the poor and homeless. He really enjoys being with people and helping others. He spends four hours there, and then spends the afternoon on the couch recuperating.

After two years of going through rehab and seeing God's grace and miracles at work, we were able to start a voluntary family support group on the ABI floor at Shepherd Center on Saturdays. When we were there, a weekend support group was not available on the ABI floor. We felt such a strong direction from God to begin one. We receive more from this group than we could ever give. The family members of those who are on the Brain Injury Unit come as they can. They love to talk to Bruce and ask a million questions about what it is like to be a brain injury patient. Seeing him doing so well brings hope to their lives and situations. My role is to encourage them from the caregiver's perspective concerning how to care for themselves and how to stand up through the stress and uncertainty. Sometimes we'll have two in our group. Sometimes we'll have twenty. They come in with fears, shock, and apprehensions. As the anxiety subsides somewhat, new friendships are forged with other family members in the unit. We all need each other, and this is a small way that Bruce and I make an effort to give back.

Bruce also goes to Pathways periodically to talk with the patients and to keep touch with those we met at Shepherd Center during our family support groups. Ann Boriskie, founder and director of the Brain Injury Peer Visitor Association in Atlanta, Georgia, made it possible for us to spend this special time at Shepherd Center on Saturdays, and we are so grateful to her for all of her efforts in this area. She is a brain injury survivor herself. After her car wreck thirteen years ago, she was not diagnosed with a brain injury until a year later. As she slowly recovered, she became driven to create a group that could help patients and families who are experiencing a TBI. Her organization now has over seventy volunteers who lead groups and make peer visits in over twenty-three hospitals and rehab centers in the Atlanta area. All the volunteers are brain injury survivors or caregivers.

Ann agrees that Bruce is a "people magnet." Everywhere he goes, whether it is at Shepherd Center, or in the grocery store, people want to talk with him and hear his story. God has been so good to open these doors and bring such good out of what has happened. Bruce always says, "God takes a mess, adds a little age to it, and gives you a message to share." He has certainly done that in our lives.

Bruce's philosophy is "invest yourself in others." Be a friend and pour your life into others. He loves to share what God has done and continues to do in his life, so others will be encouraged on their own journeys. Each day is a new adventure. God took our hand and led us the entire way, to create a totally new ministry for us. Who would have thought we would be pouring ourselves into brain injury survivors someday? He is so faithful to bring something so good out of what we perceived to be chaos—if we will only trust Him to lead the way.

BRUCE'S THOUGHTS

I passed my driving test! I never thought I would be able to drive again. Look out, world! You'll never know when I'll be in your neighborhood.

Being part of a brain injury support group is so important to me. After finishing at Pathways, one of our first outings was to find a support group. Actually, there are peer support groups all over the country. You can find them on the internet under the "Brain Injury Association of America" in your state. At our first attended meeting, I met Laura Coomes, who is the leader of the support group that meets at Kennestone Hospital, just three miles from our home. Thirty-five to forty-five brain injury survivors and their caregivers attend this gathering once a month. We all agree that things are different for us now, but in some ways, things are better.

Bruce Weiss, a stroke survivor, and I have become good friends and go to Starbucks once or twice a week. He's from Brooklyn and has a million funny stories that he tells with his strong New York accent. We laugh a lot, talk about brain injury stuff, and solve the problems of the world. It is so important for me to get out with other folks who have had similar injuries. We encourage one another. Many of those who come to our Friday morning breakfasts say, "I thought my life was over. I was very depressed, and I thought about killing myself. However, now that I've found this group, I've got a reason and a purpose for being. Friday morning is the highlight of my week. I look so forward to this breakfast."

Friday Morning Breakfasts

This has become a major part of my mission in life. Caring for brain injury survivors and navigating life together gives me fulfillment and purpose. Living in the real world with deficits can still mean experiencing life to the fullest. The criteria for those experiences have merely changed. As I've said a number of times, life is one big therapy center. I wear a T-shirt with a picture of a guy doing adaptive skit skiing with the caption, "Life is good." I truly believe life is good.

The monthly support group frequently does fun events. We often go bowling together. You haven't been bowling until you've gone with a group of brain injury survivors! It is so much fun. You might think it would be embarrassing, but we know our limitations and enjoy having fun with people who aren't judging us because of our deficits. In fact, it is quite entertaining. The first time I went bowling, I was still using a walker. Since I had no strength in my right hand, I had to bowl with my left. I reared back and let that ball fly. It bounced from side to side down the alley and went in the gutter. As I let go, my entire body twisted to the right; I looked like a tangled-up pretzel. In the middle of my "ballet," I fell in a heap on the floor. It was so hilarious. We all were laughing. They were concerned that maybe I had hit my head, but that was the only part of my body that didn't hit the floor.

I learned to laugh at myself early in this journey. A sense of humor is an essential component to getting better. Rachel gave me a T-shirt that says, "Not tonight, dear. I had brain surgery!" When I wear it to our support group, everyone has a big laugh. I learned what my limitations were, and then I tried to do some new activities—bowling, sit skiing, fishing, painting, yard work, etc. You may need to make some adaptations to make it work for you, but everyone does that in one way or another. One day, I tried golfing. Talk about hilarious! I can't hit the ball at all. I never was a very good golfer before, but now I swing about three feet away from everything I aim at. I would make a better weed whacker than a golfer. So I'll try something else.

Chapter 23

Rachel's View

As a newly hired registered nurse on the brain injury unit at Atlanta's Shepherd Center, I immediately learned I had a lot to be thankful for. I had landed a great job fresh out of nursing school, and quickly realized I had been taking many things for granted. I thanked God for our family's health each day as I worked with patients and families dealing with tremendous tragedy. With a brain injury, the injured loved one often forgets who his/her family is and what his/her role is in the family as well as experiences many emotional changes. To work with someone who does not recognize his own wife or her husband is sad. However, at Shepherd Center, we use repetition daily so the person can hopefully regain new connections in the brain and begin recovery.

When I came to my parents' home one evening, I noticed my dad's words were not coming out as he intended. He tried to type some email, but he kept typing "G" for "H" and "C" for "M," which is completely opposite from the keyboard configuration. He had trouble feeling his right side, which was very weak. Being the superhero neuro-nurse that I thought I was, I diagnosed my own father with a mild stroke. This was not to be taken lightly. As my nursing classes had drilled into me, "time is brain." I advised him to go to the doctor the next day and get a CT scan immediately. However, it took two more days before the CT scan was scheduled, which was unacceptable in my opinion. As we all know, things in the medical field do not happen as quickly as we'd like.

After Dad was admitted to the emergency room, I was floored to learn the CT scan results. My dad had two unidentifiable masses in his brain. *My* dad? Dr. Benedict said the masses appeared to be tumors. The areas might have been infections, but a normal white blood cell count and no fever completely discounted that theory. The next phase would be to perform surgery to learn if the tumors were malignant or benign.

I was shocked, to say the least. I had recently met a few people whose family members had brain cancer. Their loved ones had one surgery after another until their bodies just gave up. I didn't want my dad to suffer for years and go through that agony. I thought he'd be better off in Heaven.

When we were told Dad's surgery would be in three days, I spent as much time as possible with him. We always loved each other, but seeing him in the hospital bed, weak, and yet with a smile, made me regret not having spent more time with him before now. We always went to church together on Sunday, and this Sunday would not be any different. Dad said he would like a McDonald's sausage biscuit for breakfast, so I quickly got them. After returning to his room, I turned on our favorite TV preacher, climbed into the hospital bed, and we ate our biscuits together as we watched TV church. This was a special time for me to spend with Dad and God on the eve of his brain surgery—although I cannot remember what the sermon was about or who preached it. My mind was elsewhere. Tom Holloway, dad's lanky coworker, brought a BBQ dinner for the entire family that surgery eve. Before eating, we had a family prayer with Dr. Benedict. Everyone was there, and my grandfather thanked God for "the life that Bruce had lived and all the joy that he'd brought to us." Now, I love Papa, but this sounded like a funeral prayer to me. Dad was not dead, and I had the confidence and faith in God that he would regain his health eventually.

During surgery the next evening, I planned to go on the night shift at Shepherd Center. That may have seemed a little crazy to my family and friends. However, the day before that I spent with Dad left me with a feeling of extreme peace. Usually I'm an extremely anxious person, but I was certain God was going to handle it all. So I went on to work where I could help my patients while God took care of Dad.

The surgery was expected to last eight hours, so when my mother called three hours after the operation began, I only thought the worst. It must have ended early for a bad reason. That was my anxious nature shining through. As Mom told me the lesions were abscesses and not tumors, I was so relieved. I later learned that the abscesses of infection were encapsulated, which is why the body did not react with a fever or high white blood cell count when the tests had been done. So a second surgery had to eventually be performed to drain the second abscess. Because it was encapsulated, the antibiotics could not perforate the outer layer to kill the infection inside.

After receiving his full regimen of antibiotics, Dad was ready for rehab. The day he arrived at Shepherd Center, I knew we were blessed. I had witnessed so many great recoveries in my own patients, who had worked with this same team of doctors, therapists, and nurses, that he was going to have. However, we had to deal with first things first. Dad hadn't had a bowel movement in two weeks. His stomach was so hard and round that Dr. Kaelin ordered a nasogastric tube inserted on intermittent suction to take out the air that couldn't pass through his intestines. His stomach went down immediately, and the Foley catheter removed the backed up urine. You never realize how important excreting waste from the body is until you cannot do it.

At Shepherd Center, I watched Dad progress from a Hoyer lift to a wheelchair. His memory gradually improved, as did his vision. I have had patients whose discharge dates were extended for more therapy, but Dad was the first I had seen to have his discharge date moved up to come home sooner than expected. As Dr. Kaelin said, "His recovery has been miraculous."

In outpatient therapy, I saw him improve from the wheelchair, to a walker, to a cane, and then to a simple boot to wear inside his shoe. I learned so much from being on the other side of the picture that I am now more aware of what the families as well as the patients are going through. It has made me a much better nurse. Tragedy can happen to anyone, any day, and any time. Cherish every moment that you have to experience life with your family and friends.

An important concept for families and caregivers to understand is that therapy should not stop when the patient returns home. As the saying goes, "Use it or lose it." A brain injury victim is not automatically healed just because they have been discharged from rehabilitation. The new challenges every day should be met to stimulate the mind. These can be simple activities such as going out to eat. Adding a tip to a restaurant bill was difficult for Dad, but it was an important skill to develop to keep his mind working as it created new pathways for emerging memories.

When Dad was released from his official outpatient therapy, my work schedule was perfect for us to spend some time together. I worked the night shift, and Dad needed someone to drive him places so he wouldn't be home alone all day while Mom was at work. We ate lunch every day and ran errands together. This special time together benefited both of us.

I had learned from the therapists not to do and answer everything for him. For example, when he was at home, he'd say, "Laura, I'm thirsty." He would then wait for her to get a drink for him. (He was so used to everyone waiting on him in the hospital.) I had learned that if his legs can operate, he should get the drink himself. He experienced physical therapy as he walked to the refrigerator and occupational therapy as he found the glass, put ice in, and poured the beverage of his choice. It took a while for him to get used to waiting on himself, but when I heard him say, "I'm going to get a drink. Do you want something?" I realized another milestone had been reached.

Dad strengthened daily and went to the gym a few times a week. He practiced reading the paper, which was very confusing for him due to his visual deficits. He would get to the bottom of one column, but would not be able to find where the next column began at the top.

With much determination, practice, and improvement, I am proud to say Dad was able to perform my wedding ceremony this year, *and* walk me down the aisle as I had always imagined. It was an amazing day, not only for my new husband and me, but also for Dad. He was able to read the entire sermon and ceremony without stumbling over one word. The father-daughter dance at the reception was, if I may say so myself, the best dance ever done!

Photo courtesy of MikeMoonStudio.com

Father-daughter dance at Rachel's wedding

Chapter 24

Personal Stories from Other Brain Injury Survivors

An estimated 1.7 million Americans suffer an acquired or traumatic brain injury each year (see Appendix F). Many of these will experience some degree of recovery, but coming back to the people they once were is gradual and uncertain. These patients are entering a lifelong period of possible attention, concentration, memory, fatigue, cognitive, and emotional deficits. Their lives are forever change by their injuries, but they are not without hope.

Accepting and finding their "new normal" is as important as regaining cognitive skills. We have asked some of our brain injury survivor friends to briefly share their stories of struggles, deficits, and adaptations to their current way of life. Brain injuries can happen in a variety of ways: a car wreck, motorcycle accident, fall, stroke, tumor, assault, or being hit in the head. The following are true stories of how some other brain injury survivors deal with their "new normal."

David Keller, 49, Georgia
Diagnosed with Meningioma
September 15, 2010

My wife, Leigh, and I had married and created a blended family with five children—all girls—less than six months before I was diagnosed with a meningioma brain tumor. Starting a new home has enough challenges of its own without having everything stopped in its tracks by a tumor. A few months before the wedding, my right eye began to droop, so the eye doctor prescribed glasses. After the wedding, there were more noticeable changes such as fatigue, lack of interest in exercising, headaches, and changes in my attitude. I was almost like a different person.

In September 2010, I made an appointment with the doctor for my yearly checkup. After I explained my concerns, he did an MRI, and the tumor was discovered. This was later confirmed by a neurosurgeon. The surgery was scheduled for the next month, and the doctors were able to remove 90% of the plum-size tumor. They said it could have been growing for over twenty years.

A meningioma is a tumor that develops in the meninges, the tissue that surrounds and protects the brain and spinal cord. Although most tumors of this type are not cancerous, a meningioma can cause problems as it grows and presses against important parts of the brain or spinal cord, such as the optic nerve sheath, which protects the nerve connecting the eye to the brain. This was my situation.

During the surgery, I experienced a venous stroke that affected the frontal lobe of my brain. This area controls the emotions, actions, and reasoning. When I woke up, I had some definite deficits in these functions. I spent seven days in the hospital before beginning outpatient treatment at the WellStar Rehab Clinic, where I continued therapy for three months. My treatment included work with an occupational therapist, speech therapist, neuropsychologist, and a physical therapist.

In July 2011, when I began seeing a radiologist, the cyber knife radiation treatment was administered to kill the remaining cells surrounding the main artery feeding my brain. This could not have been surgically removed during the first operation because it would have cost me my life.

The original tumor damaged my right eye. Now I must wait for the radiation treatment to heal, and then I will undergo two more surgeries to correct the damage to the third optic nerve and muscles. Doctors will continue to care for me for another year or so.

Initially, my deficits and challenges were many. I had lost all of my cognitive skills, so I had to relearn simple things like:

- Chewing with my mouth closed

- Walking and looking up, not at my feet

- Cooking and taking care of the kids

- Expressing emotional feelings

- Balancing the check book

- Compensating for the peripheral vision loss on my left side

- Dealing with large crowds and loud music or sounds

- Dealing with short-term memory loss (but I could remember everything from the past)

My new family was definitely the focus of my motivation as I did my therapy daily. I needed to provide a stable environment for my three little girls. I also needed to learn how to care for and help raise them. I believe I progressed faster because of my strong desire to function with my family again. Since my wife and I had been married less than six months, we needed to rebuild our home and family. This stroke took us back to before our beginning, and we knew, together with God's support, we would make it, but it was not an easy road.

I am very dedicated to my work as a telecom field support staff member, and I really wanted to get back to work. During rehab, I never gave up or felt defeated, and I continually looked for ways to accomplish and do more. However, my return to work five months after surgery was extremely hard on my recovery. I went back too early and should have taken a few more months to recover. My brain was overloaded, and I was exhausted each day. I have been gaining more stamina over the past few months, and now I am taking fewer naps. It will be months, if not years, before I will be where I was prior to the stroke. I am experiencing and understanding this statement.

God continues to strengthen my wife, Leigh, and me every step of the way through this experience. Without the faith that He granted us, we would have fallen apart and would not have been able to achieve all that we have. I still have some difficulties with short-term memory, peripheral blockage in my left side vision, and an inability to reason through some challenges. However, as we move forward, I believe those will continue to improve.

People are stronger than they believe they are. When I was put in a situation and had to break through the barriers, I did it—but not alone. I've learned that there is always someone else who has more challenges than I do. Don't dwell on the negative, but rather focus on the progress made. With God's help, anything can be achieved.

Life is what you make of it. No matter what happens to you, keep your head held up high. God has a purpose for everyone in this life. It is up to us to make sure we are fulfilling that purpose. Don't allow life to slip by without taking advantage of your situations. If this had not happened to me, we would not have met so many wonderful new friends. For that, we are truly blessed. Leigh and I have grown closer as a couple. I knew she was my soul mate, but until this happened, I didn't realize how much we needed each other. Our frustrations grew, our anger grew, and our love bloomed and overpowered all of the negatives. Hope, faith, and love.

Leigh and David Keller, Nancy Ward and Clem Suder

Clem Suder, 54, Georgia
Fell Down the Stairs
May 16, 2006

I got up in the middle of the night for some reason. We have never figured out why, but I think it was to take my blood pressure medicine. As I came down the stairs, I passed out and fell—landing face down on the hardwood floor. My son was home and heard the fall. He found me unconscious at the bottom of the stairs and thought I was passed out drunk, so he put a pillow under my head and left me there. Nancy, my caregiver, was in Florida with her family. The next day, my son said I was not acting "right," and he called an ambulance, but I refused treatment. I could name the current president, but not my own son. If I answered enough questions right, I knew the paramedics could not make me go to the hospital. Finally, two days after the accident, some of my friends tricked me into going to the hospital.

At first, the doctors thought I had suffered a stroke, but later they decided I just passed out. The x-rays showed I had suffered a trauma to the front left side of my brain, where there was swelling and bleeding. It was a week before I realized I had double vision. The damage was already done, so I received no medication. I cannot emphasize enough the importance of getting treatment immediately after a brain trauma so treatment can begin quickly.

I spent two weeks in rehabilitation at Kennestone Hospital in Marietta, Georgia. I had no memory of the accident, or Nancy. As I looked around the hospital room one night, she asked if I knew where I was. After much thought, I said, "On a cruise?" When she told me I was in the hospital, I said, "Thank God. This would be the crappiest room for a cruise!" Nancy and I had known each other for six years, but we had only officially been dating for two months when the accident happened. I have no memory of her before the accident. That's sad for her, but she has six years of memories, which she tells me about frequently.

As rehab began, I had balance issues and was not allowed to walk without a nurse holding the wide belt around my waist for stability. Besides balance, memory was another major problem. Re-learning how to read, spell, and develop hand-eye coordination were all great challenges. Tossing bean bags into a bucket really frustrated me. Brushing my teeth, shaving, and combing my hair were difficult tasks, but I kept after those activities and developed the skills once again. When I was released from the hospital, I spent a few more months in out-patient rehabilitation.

Before my fall, I was the regional service manager for a dental company. I managed nine men who loved and respected me. My company was wonderful to me. I had great insurance, and following my rehabilitation, I went back to work. After about two months, my boss told me to take some time off, go back to the doctors, and make sure I was able to work. At that time, I had no memory of the day before, so each day was a blank page. I didn't tell Nancy, so no one knew—or so I thought. I knew I wasn't right, but I wanted to be "normal" again. I thought if I went to work, the memories would all come back to me. They didn't. I never went back to work after that attempt. I have long-term disability, so I am officially retired now.

Learning to live with my deficits has been my biggest challenge. I am continually trying to find out who the new "me" is, and what and why I believe as I do about life. I have extremely limited memory. It's not that it is not there at all, but I cannot access it like before, even when prompted with specifics. Without my short-term memory, the smallest routine of daily living can become amazingly difficult, and being a contributing member to society becomes extremely difficult, if not impossible. I cannot think through what plans I need to make for the day. I also get tired to the point of being unable to process new information. I become confused extremely quickly. I do not consistently recognize landmarks, and consequently get lost very easily. I still become physically tired which can and does lead to balance problems. Multi-tasking does not happen.

Nancy, my caregiver, has been by my side since the injury. I couldn't have recovered like I have without her. The brain does far more than I ever knew or thought about. It has an amazing ability to repair itself and go on. I spend my time doing the things I enjoy and being with my friends. One day a week I work at MUST Ministries. I'm involved in a brain injury support group of about forty-five people, which is very important to me. I learn a lot from them, and we have a good time together. Having a social network is so important. I am a motorcycle biker, so Nancy and I take short rides with friends when the weather is good. I have a great group of biker friends with whom we ride once in a while, and they remind me about the things we did in the "good old days." Times like that help to slowly build back my memory. I love Nancy's family, and we do a lot of things with her sisters and our families as well.

I have learned that we take much of our everyday life and interaction for granted. We assume that everyone we meet doesn't have a problem with performing normal, daily functions. I used to believe that what we are is based on what we do. However, life is much more than that—we are who we are because of who we are—not because of what we do for a living. We define ourselves through our own actions. It's not so important what we do, but how we live with what we are.

Bruce, Kelly Campbell, and Laura

Kelly Campbell, Single Mother, 41, Georgia
Suffered a Stroke
July 9, 2009

My journey through a brain injury actually began before birth. After my stroke in 2009, I learned that I had a genetic disorder called fibro-muscular dysplasia (FMD). FMD is a condition in which an abnormal cluster of cells grows in the artery wall of at least one artery. The artery narrows and can form clots that travel to other parts of the body—in my case, to my brain. This caused my stroke, which left me completely paralyzed on the left side. Thankfully and amazingly, I had no cognitive or speech deficits, so my mind is fine, but my body is a daily challenge.

I was initially treated at Emory University Hospital for eight days, and then spent six weeks in the in-patient rehabilitation unit at WellStar Cobb Hospital in Austell, Georgia. I knew my left side was paralyzed, but the reality of my situation wasn't truly clear until that first day in rehab. The physical therapist came in with a wheelchair and helped me transfer from the bed to the chair. That simple act hit me so hard that I began to cry and cried the entire session. I sent my closest friend a text message that read, "I'm in a wheelchair. I want to die."

Over the next six weeks, I realized that my physical issues were much worse than most stroke survivors, but my lack of cognitive or speech issues was a true blessing. However, physically I was hit hard, and despite my hard work, I left the rehab center completely non-ambulatory, unable to walk or even stand on my own.

Out-patient rehab occupied most of my time for the next year. My left side was completely paralyzed, so I was unable to return to my home alone. My brother and his wife willingly took me into their home. Including their four children, there were seven of us in a three-bedroom, two-bathroom house. The doors were not wide enough for my wheelchair to maneuver, and going to the restroom took *seven* transfers between the wheelchair to a regular chair to the toilet and back. The first week was tough, learning to adjust to my new body. It took over a month to get strong enough to use a walker and not the wheelchair in the house, and eight weeks before I could even dress myself without help.

Another difficult adjustment was not having my two boys living with me. They lived twenty miles away with their dad, and I only saw them every other weekend. I was unable to drive for the first fourteen months following the stroke, so I was dependent on others to go anywhere or to see my boys. They were my inspiration—I had to do all I could to get as well as I could for them. I realized early on that if I chose to be bitter and angry, I would never get better. My own attitude was pivotal in my recovery.

After spending the first ten months with my brother and family, I moved in with my father and stepmother as a transition to independent living. Three months later, I began to drive again (which opened the world to me) and soon moved out to be on my own. I have lived alone since February 2011, and I am now only a mile from my boys, so I can see them much more often.

Currently I have no use of my left arm at all and very limited use of my left leg. I can walk with a cane, but I struggle when I am out in the community as uneven surfaces and steep ramps are extremely difficult for me to manage. I have gotten stuck in places where the sidewalk ramp was too steep for me to walk down and have had to ask strangers to help me step off the curb. I can live alone with the help of adaptive equipment in the kitchen and bathroom.

The lessons I have learned from this experience are vast and varied. I know God didn't cause my stroke, but He knew it was coming and was with me every step of the way. He knew that nothing would be harder for me than having to give up control and be totally dependent on others. Learning to be transparent and being willing to let others in was difficult but necessary for me to grow. My critical spirit had already cost me my marriage and kept me from forming strong, healthy relationships. Having to rely on others to do everything for me took care of that very quickly. It's not smart to criticize those who literally hold your life in their hands.

Today I can honestly say I am healthier physically, emotionally, mentally, spiritually, and financially than before my stroke. I am certainly a better mother and friend as I take time to listen and not stay in constant motion. Life is a challenge physically as I still have no use of my left arm and very limited use of my leg, but I focus on the fact that I can walk, even if it's with a cane. I remember that first day in the wheelchair and realize how far I've come. Today, I spend time reading, doing Bible studies, and visiting friends and family. I'm the go-to babysitter for my nieces and nephew, and I am a huge part of my boys' lives. I am blessed indeed!

Darrel Williams and Bruce

Darrel Williams, 57, Alabama
Fell Off a Fire Truck
December 29, 2007

Entering retirement was an exciting time for me. I had been a forklift truck driver for US Gypsum Company, and I was ready for a slower pace. I was now going to be a volunteer with our fire department. Two months after joining, I was going on my first house fire call. When I heard the radio, I grabbed my gear and drove to the station. Standing on the back of the fire truck, I started to put on my suit, but the truck rolled forward. I fell backward off the truck onto the asphalt. The driver didn't know I was there. 911 was called immediately when the other volunteers noticed that the right side of my head had taken quite a blow.

I don't remember much of what happened. I spent four weeks at Erlanger in Chattanooga where a large portion of my skull was removed to give the brain room to swell. My skull was put

130

in the freezer for safekeeping, and I went to a nursing home for three weeks. My wife, Karen, then made arrangements for me to be transferred to Shepherd Center in Atlanta for rehab. After the swelling of the brain went down, I looked like someone had hit me in the head with a large bowling ball. I wore a helmet to protect my brain.

For two months, I was at Shepherd Center for inpatient therapy, and then at Pathways for outpatient rehab for a few more months. Learning to walk, talk, and recognize people were my biggest obstacles at first. My family was there to support me, but I didn't recognize them for about six weeks. Karen had to bathe and shave me until I was able to do those skills again.

My greatest ambition was to drive my truck again. At Pathways, I was told it would be five more months before I could even consider driving. As I went home June 20, 2008, I was ready to find a facility that would teach me to drive again. I found Siskin Hospital for Physical Rehabilitation in Chattanooga, and started my outpatient rehab there. When the day came for my driver's evaluation, I was ready! The therapist let me drive on all types of streets. At the end of the session, she approved me for driving and notified all of the necessary parties—including my wife, Karen. As we headed home, Karen drove. She wasn't quite ready to let me loose in downtown Chattanooga yet.

Six months after the accident, the doctors at Erlanger said it was time to put my skull back in. They told me they could finally put Humpty Dumpty together again. Surgery involved 157 staples, but at least I didn't need my helmet any longer.

Problems that I deal with now revolve mostly around how quickly I can get things done. I'm much slower at completing jobs because the concentration that I need takes longer. What used to take three hours now takes a couple of days to finish.

However, moving slower has its advantages. I need to be slower to play with my five grandbabies, who occupy a lot of my time. I love my grandchildren and spend every minute I can with them. I also bush hog, mow the grass, go to church, and go fishing. I hook the bush hog up to my tractor and help a few neighbors with their property. My church and pastor were very supportive in praying for me, as were friends from all over the country. I have a stronger faith in God and what He can do after going through this experience. Things have been tight financially since I'm on Social Security Disability now, but I'm grateful for that help. We sold our four-wheelers, but after having brain surgery, I don't suppose I need them anymore!

Bruce and Scott McEvoy

Scott McEvoy, 58, Florida
Beaten and Left for Dead
January 26, 2008

As I drove up to my house, I noticed the light was on in the garage. That seemed odd, especially since I had been gone for the past ten days, but my neighbors had a key and checked on my mail and newspapers, so I brushed it off. After pulling into the garage, I entered the house door. I took two steps inside and was immediately confronted by a man pointing a gun at me. "If you do what I say, you'll live." The next six hours were a nightmare. I didn't try to resist him because I wanted to live.

Since I had no jewelry and only $125 in my pocket, the man tied my hands behind me, put me in the back seat of my car, and drove me to eight or nine different ATMs, where he forced me to withdraw $100 at each. Each time, he untied my hands so I could work the ATM, but he kept a gun pointed at me. This went on for a few hours. At the last bank, I purposely dropped my card to the ground and told him that the machine ate it.

The man was aware that I had a house in Jacksonville, Florida, which was one and a half hours away by car. We drove there that night. I thought I could get help at the gate to the community, but the infrared eye read the sticker on my bumper and opened the gate. We spent an hour at my house while he looked for jewels and money. We then drove back to Ormond Beach, where he had left his "stuff" at my beach house. He tied my arms behind my back very securely, which was very painful. I begged him to loosen the rope a bit to ease the pain in my shoulder. To my surprise, he did. He then wrapped my head tightly in Saran Wrap to suffocate me. I managed to position my chin so I had a pocket of air and could breathe a little. He left me in the room alone while he went to steal things from neighboring houses. When he returned, he realized I wasn't dead, so he pistol whipped me a number of times in the head until I was unconscious. He thought then I was dead, so he loaded up his stolen stash in my Cadillac and drove away.

After lying unconscious in a pool of blood for about thirty minutes, I woke up and was able to partly untie myself. If he had not loosened the rope earlier, I would not have been able to free myself. I picked up a mobile phone, but I couldn't dial it. I crawled out of the house and managed to drag myself about a block to a large intersection. Sadly, no one stopped to help. I was covered in blood and looked terrible. Finally an off-duty officer from the sheriff's department and his wife stopped and called 911. The ambulance took me to Halifax Hospital, and brain surgery was performed immediately due to the swelling that had already occurred.

When the assailant stole my Cadillac that night, he torched it in Daytona Beach. We learned he had been in my house for several days, storing the loot that he had been stealing from other houses. He was eventually traced to Miami where, while he was shoplifting, he shot and killed a CVS employee. When the police confronted him, he turned the gun on himself and committed suicide.

I spent two weeks in the hospital and five weeks at in-patient rehab at Peninsula Rehabilitation Center in Daytona Beach. I couldn't walk, talk, or get to the bathroom on my own, but I always knew my girlfriend, Paula. She arranged for me to do my out-patient therapy at Shepherd Pathways in Atlanta for four months. The therapists at both rehab facilities were very encouraging. As I approached each new challenge, they would say, "You can do this!" I also went to Brooks Rehabilitation Center in Jacksonville, Florida, for several more months of therapy. Having a goal or challenge kept me pressing toward the mark.

Today my right side is still numb, and my peripheral vision is also affected. I really wanted to drive a car again, and after a year, I was able to reach that goal. I am more methodical and slow in what I attempt now, and I drive very carefully. If I feel rushed, my processor doesn't work as well, so I try not to rush. I haven't had a seizure in three years, so my next challenge is to fly again. I was an airline pilot before the attack, and to be reinstated with the FAA is my heart's desire.

My thinking is slower, and my memory is not as good. I write everything down. I can get confused and frustrated easily. My patience is not what it used to be. Paula asks the people around me to be patient, and that helps. I ask God every day to help me to get through each step. I go to the gym frequently to work out and exercise my brain and body. We do crossword puzzles, math problems, and play cards.

Even though my life has changed, I have learned to compensate in my activities to live a full life. My advice to someone with a brain injury is to never give up. There is always hope on the horizon. Don't put limits on yourself. Be aware of your deficits, but push yourself. Try to do anything that you'd like to do. Live your life by the Golden Rule—treat others like you want to be treated.

Laura Coomes, Mother, 27, North Carolina
Suffered a Stroke
September 24, 2003

After having had severe headaches for two days, I was at work but unable to get much done due to the pain. I worked as a financial analyst for a company, and my job required my full attention, preferably without pain. I had experienced headaches all my life, but the doctors said the headaches were like migraines, even though I never had the normal symptoms that come from migraines. I decided to go home early from work that day to get some relief. A co-worker asked me to quickly help her with a project as I was heading out the door. When I leaned on her desk, I had a full stroke. I couldn't talk, walk, or move my body. It was like I was frozen all over, but I was conscious.

Someone called 911, and within two minutes the paramedics arrived. All I could think about was Griffin, our seven-month-old son. Who was going to pick him up at daycare? Who was going to take care of him if his mommy is sick? I remember being wheeled out of the office on a gurney, and then I lost consciousness. I vaguely woke up as we were on the elevator going to the ambulance. However, I have no recollection of anything from then on for the next six and a half weeks. After being put into a drug-induced coma for two weeks, I was awakened. The first one I wanted to see after I kissed my husband, Bryan, was our son, Griffin. I don't remember anything that happened during those first few weeks. The doctors' diagnosis was a cerebral arteriovenous malformation (AVM), which is an abnormal connection between the arteries and veins in the brain that usually forms before birth. I had an AVM rupture that resulted in bleeding in my brain. This occurs in less than 1% of people. As a result of the rupture, I had multiple hemorrhagic strokes over the course of the next hour.

Moses H. Cone Memorial Hospital in Greensboro, North Carolina, was my home for the next three months—five weeks in ICU, and two months at inpatient rehab. Therapy was a challenge for me both mentally and physically, but I had to get better to care for my family. Griffin and Bryan were definitely my driving inspiration and motivation to get as well as I could. One of the most memorable days in the hospital was when, after two months, the doctor pulled out my feeding tube. He said, "This will only hurt a little." His definition of hurt and my definition are miles apart!

I had no memory of what had happened, but after five months, things started to slowly come back. Going home, I was scared and nervous that if I needed someone with professional services, they wouldn't be available, but everything turned out fine. I spent six months in outpatient therapy and have continued therapy even today.

Eight months after my stroke, I tried to go back to work. I had always been a busy, active, productive person, and I thought that would be the normal thing to do. I started working one hour a week, doing easy jobs like checking email. Then it was increased to five, to ten, and then to fifteen hours a week. When I tried to work twenty hours per week, I struggled to get any work done at all. I made many mistakes and was very frustrated. However, two years after my stroke, Bryan got a job offer in Atlanta, so we moved to the Atlanta area. Being a mommy became my full-time job.

Caring for a two-and-a-half-year-old is hard when you are physically and mentally able. When you have a brain injury, it is even harder. My right side doesn't function at 100%, so simple tasks like holding him, preparing food, and bathing him were difficult, but I adapted and did what I could with what I had. Caring for him was harder for me mentally than physically. I couldn't give him my full attention because I had to be conscious of the care I needed as well as the care he needed. I couldn't play on the floor with him like I used to, but I adapted by playing on the bed.

Today I still have difficulty with short-term memory. Note taking is invaluable, except sometimes I forget where I put my notes. I don't handle stress and pressure well, so even though I am always busy, I try to stay calm. My stamina is definitely not what it used to be. I tire easily, and I have to give in and rest so I can go again. My right foot is called a drop foot—it doesn't stay in position to walk on its own. It flops, so I had to wear an ankle-foot orthosis (AFO) brace for a long time. Now I have a brace that fits around my ankle and foot to hold my foot in position as I walk. My right arm has about 85% of its normal strength and use. I also have a pride problem. I don't like to ask anyone for help. I want to do it all on my own, which is not always possible.

With a brain injury, I learned to adapt to activities and found that life can still be fulfilling. I took a driving evaluation, and I am now able to drive everywhere. However, I do carry a card explaining my deficits if it is ever needed. I frequently go to the gym to exercise the weak parts of my body—which sometimes feels like every part. I coordinate the "Unlimited Possibilities" Support Group for Brain Injury Survivors that meets once a month. More than forty people have a great time sharing what we have learned about living in the "new normal." We often have speakers who help us understand topics such as Social Security Disability, Medicare, or how to set up a trust. We frequently have psychologists interact with us, and even had a Tae Kwon Do instructor teach us how to defend ourselves.

Many people from this group also meet for breakfast each Friday morning at the Whistlestop Café, where we eat and share in a good time together. This group ranges from ten to thirty-five people each Friday. It is the high point of our week.

Volunteer work is fulfilling as I help others along the way. I do peer visitation with families and patients who are hospitalized with a brain injury. I feel it is so important to give encouragement to those who are just starting on this difficult journey.

Realize that every day is a blessing. Remember: if you want it, it can happen. Don't let anybody tell you that you can't do something, if you think and know you can.

Bruce Weiss, Denise Bourne, Ken and Ronda Prokop, and Laura Coomes

Ken Prokop, 49, Pennsylvania
Car Wreck
March 6, 2009

I have no recollection of my accident. In fact, I don't remember anything from March 6, 2009, to early May 2009. The following is an account that my family, friends, and doctors have told me.

On a beautiful Friday morning, I was driving home from running errands before my work day began. As I crossed an intersection approximately two miles from my home, I was T-boned on the driver's side by a Waste Management (Mack) Roll-Off garbage truck. I was unconscious at the scene of the accident, and it took twenty-five minutes for the rescue workers to remove me from my Jeep Grand Cherokee. My fourteen-year-old daughter, Sarah, can fill in the gaps:

> "This can't be my dad," I thought to myself over and over again as I looked down at the body of my father. The strongest man I knew was lying in a hospital bed with machines keeping him alive. I couldn't understand how someone who could build a house, build a life, and build a family could be lying there incapable of building a breath.

I was evacuated by air to the Neuroscience Trauma Unit of Lehigh Valley Cedarcrest Hospital in Allentown, Pennsylvania. That was my home for the next month. As I lay in a comatose state, the doctors gave my family the devastating diagnosis. I had suffered a severe traumatic brain injury—damage to the frontal lobe and a diffuse axonal injury (DAI). With a DAI, the damage to the brain occurs over a large area, which is one of the major causes of unconsciousness and long-term coma after a traumatic brain injury. In severe DAI, the patient may never regain consciousness. Besides having this bleak future looming ahead, I also had suffered nine broken ribs, a bruised heart, multiple fractures of my spine and both pelvic bones, a lacerated spleen, a large head wound, a paralyzed vocal cord, and fluid on my lungs. I remained in a coma about two weeks.

Exactly one month after the accident, I was transported to Kessler Institute for Rehabilitation in Chester, New Jersey. There I began my speech, occupational, physical, and cognitive therapies for six weeks of inpatient and then four months as an outpatient. During that time, I relearned to walk, talk, eat, and challenge my brain.

Due to mounting expenses and my lost income, we had to sell our home in the Poconos. On October 2, 2009, we moved to Atlanta, Georgia, to be near Shepherd Center and my father. I continued my therapy three days a week at Shepherd Pathways until late February 2010. In all, I had almost twelve months of inpatient and outpatient care. I still continue my therapy at home even today.

After waking from the coma, I measured a "3" on the Glasgow Coma Scale (see Appendix G) which measures levels of consciousness after a brain injury on a scale of one to fifteen. If I were to miraculously survive, given the odds, I would live the rest of my days in a vegetative state. After two days of consciousness, I challenged my doctors, nurses, and family even more as my blood pressure skyrocketed and then plummeted. My body temperature was over 104 degrees, which caused the doctors to place me on a bed of ice for two weeks. I had spontaneous episodes of cardiac arrhythmia (the heart beats too fast, too slow, or with irregular rhythms) and profuse sweating. My family couldn't believe I was facing more challenges to survive.

I was also suffering a reaction to my severe brain injury known as storming. Symptoms of storming can include changes in the level of consciousness, increased posturing, dystonia, hypertension, hyperthermia, tachycardia, tachypnea, diaphoresis, and agitation. A patient who experiences storming is "at a low level of neurological activity with minimal alertness, minimal awareness, and reflexive motor response to stimulation, and the storming can take a seemingly peaceful individual into a state of chaos."[8]

---

[8] Denise M. Lemke, "Riding Out the Storm: Sympathetic Storming after Traumatic Brain Injury," *The Journal of Neuroscience Nursing*, 36, no. 1 (2004).

The respirator kept me alive, a feeding tube provided my nutrition, and a chest tube removed the fluid from my lungs. However, my family never gave up hope and never stopped praying. I later learned prayer chains were held for me across the country. About two weeks later, I began squeezing the hands that held mine and answering questions with a thumbs up. I soon opened my eyes. Though I could not speak yet, hope was restored in the hearts and minds of my family and friends.

My inspiration and motivation to try to recover was my family—the most important thing in my life. I wanted to pull through for them. My wife, Ronda, my son, Stephen, and my daughter, Sarah, were and have been there for me in the dark days and the continuing days of recovery. I also don't believe I would be here today if it were not for God in my life. I had a strong desire and will to live, just like before the accident. I kept fighting and never gave up. Will and determination are vital to anyone's recovery.

Now that I am three years out from my accident, I still experience some deficits that are slowly improving but are still very present. These include memory loss, emotional problems, headaches, depression, neuropathy, unsteady balance and fatigue, dysarthria, swallowing problems, vision, and hearing loss. I am always cold on my left side. The brain has difficulty regulating my body temperature. I constantly wear a glove on my left hand to keep it warm. My family says I look like Michael Jackson!

Even with these changes to my normal routine, I have come to realize that life is precious and fragile. One instant—one second—can change your life forever. Appreciate what you have when you have it. Never say never. Don't ever give up. Find a support group of people who have experienced a similar situation. It is so important to realize you are not alone in this new way of life. I was truly blessed with the amazing medical and rehabilitation care I received, a loving family, and the grace of God. Don't ever take the little things in life for granted.

Denise Bourne, 27, Georgia
Hit in the Head by a Crosstie
May 22, 1987

I was swinging in our old family swing at my parents' place with my two little nieces one afternoon. The swing had a crossbar, made from a railroad crosstie, about seven feet off the ground. It was an old swing, and as it collapsed, the crosstie fell and hit me directly in the head. My niece walked to the house and calmly told Grandma that the swing had fallen. "Was anyone hurt?" She replied, "Yes, Denise." My mother rushed to the swing to find me bleeding profusely from the huge gash in my head.

I saw lots of dots, but I never passed out. Blood was dripping everywhere, so my dad took me to the hospital emergency room for some stitches. As the doctors asked me questions, I didn't know the answers—where do you work, what is your name, etc. Then paralysis started taking over my body piece by piece. I passed out and had a grand mal seizure. That had never happened to me before. When I woke up, I couldn't move my arms. Following a CT scan, the doctors found that I had a hole in my skull and would need brain surgery. They sewed up my head and sent me to a larger hospital for surgery.

The doctors at Kennestone Hospital rushed me into the operating room for surgery because they said in another fifteen minutes, I would be dead. They had to clean debris and blood out my brain's frontal lobe along with repairing it. After five days in the hospital, I was sent home to go on living my life. Friends came to visit, but from the look on their faces when they saw me, I knew I looked awful. In 1987, rehabilitation wasn't available. I simply went home to recover. I had recently bought a new home next door to my brother, so that's where I lived. My young nieces and nephews took turns coming over to stay with me at night, but they were the nearest thing I had to a caregiver. My mother paid a driver to take me to places I needed to go.

Never mentioning any of my daily problems, I moved on through life. I never told *anyone* of the struggles I was experiencing. Seizures continued along with headaches. However, after two years, I was able to drive again. Three years after the accident, I had the added responsibility of two little boys to raise. I was afraid that if I told anyone about my deficits, the authorities would take my boys away from me, so I kept quiet. I was a good mother. If I was cold, I knew the kids were cold and cared for them. I couldn't process information, and my memory was gone. Before this happened, I had been preparing to get my doctorate in pastoral care. However, now the doctor said that was no longer a possibility.

I worked at our family business where I would show up but not really accomplish much. I was clumsy and made many mistakes. Constantly people asked, "What's wrong with you? Why are you such a screw-up? Why can't you do that?" My parents seemed to overlook the obvious—I had a brain injury— but that wasn't really addressed in those days. My brothers didn't really care except when I was in the way. I was really embarrassed about my situation.

Processing organizational skills is still very difficult for me today. I do not deal with money or paying bills. I get easily overwhelmed by pressure in my life which, in turn, causes seizures. I don't experience grand mal seizures any more, but I still have regular ones frequently. My brain feels like it is hurting when I read. Reading is a slow process, and I don't retain anything that I read. I remember things that happened before the accident, but I have no short-term memory. I can't remember what happened yesterday or this morning. I have my iPhone, iPad, and computer on which I can make notes, remind myself of appointments, and keep track of my life instead of having to remember everything.

Aphasia (mixing up my words) is still a part of my thinking. I experience social anxiety and can become very dependent on others. I have to obsess over tasks until they get done, because

I forget them so easily. Time means nothing to me. Life runs together. My brothers watch out for me now. They handle all of my money issues and protect their sister.

The best thing that I have learned from this experience is that having a support group is imperative. I used to think that I was all alone and that no one else was facing the difficulties that I was. When I joined the brain injury support group, I found a lot of people who were having similar experiences, and we learned from each other about how to improve our lives. I don't need a cane. I don't physically have trouble getting around, but I certainly enjoy having friends now who understand me. I've traveled this road alone long enough.

Bruce Weiss, 57, New York
Suffered a Stroke
November 15, 2008

I woke up with poor balance, but I was used to this because of my disconnected right leg quad muscle. This particular day, the balance was worse than usual. I took a hot shower, which helped somewhat, and went to the bagel store for coffee. My words seemed to slur when I ordered. As I drove my car to run an errand, I noticed that I was almost rear-ending each car in front. In a store, the clerk said he could not understand me because of my garbled speech. I thought he was mistaken, but then I noticed I had trouble signing my credit card receipt. By the time I got home, I felt terrible. I was tired, grouchy, confused, had a headache, experienced ringing in my ears, and hurt in every joint in my body.

Claudia, my wife, had gone shopping, but as I tried to call her, I could not remember the phone number, nor could I dial the phone. Going to a neighbor for assistance never occurred to me. I took a shower, had a beer, and went to bed thinking that I was just overly tired. When Claudia arrived home, I still could not communicate, so she called our doctor, who said I probably had a stroke and needed to get to the hospital as soon as possible.

I spent ten days in the hospital and five weeks in rehab. Many challenges presented themselves at the onset: speech (stuttering), poor balance, confusion, aphasia, staggered walking, weakness on the right side, and extreme fatigue. I had enough stubbornness left to not give up fighting against what had happened. When the doctors said I could not do something, I'd ask, "Why?" I never wanted to be a burden to anybody, especially my wife and kids, so I continued to fight. My brother had died the year before with an aortic dissection, and he had no opportunity to fight. I felt like I have been given another chance, and I was going for it.

As my smaller strokes continued, the doctor discovered a hole in my heart that had been there since birth. Apparently, clots were being released, which caused me to have mini-strokes during the past few years. Surgery was performed recently on my heart, and hopefully I won't have any more strokes.

Today, Claudia is my caregiver and continues to look for new ways to help me with my disabilities. I know she hates to see me struggle with mobility and cognitive issues, but she has always been there and always will be.

After almost four years of rehab and doctors, I continue to have problems with balance, walking, fatigue, making correct decisions, double vision, pain, and ringing in my ears. I have no tolerance for stupidity; unfortunately, the gates in my brain are completely down, so I tend to say what I think, which is sometimes embarrassing to my wife, but not me. I also have time management issues.

When a brain injury enters your life, you have the opportunity to learn many things that affect how you should live. Here is some advice from my experiences:

First, don't be afraid to challenge doctors or fire them and hire others. Be honest with them, and bring someone with you whom you trust to listen during the doctor visits. Challenge all medical fees, especially the hospital charges. Mistakes are always in their favor.

Often people who you thought were your friends may choose to not be part of your life any longer. I think many of them cannot handle your problems, so they don't call or come to visit.

It's important to join a support group and be involved with it as much as you can. If none exists, start your own. Search the internet for the Brain Injury Association in your state and find a group that meets near you.

Don't be ashamed to give in to the fatigue and rest every day. I don't always do this, which results in problems for me.

Continue going to therapy and, above all, keep moving your body and working with the doctors and therapists.

Find a church or temple you like and consider becoming a member. They usually have activities that can help you develop new friendships and keep you socially involved.

Unless you are rich, tell the hospital and doctors that they are going to have to wait for their payment. Set up a payment plan with the provider. Don't let them intimidate you.

Finally, try not to strain the relationships you have with your family and friends. I have such a renewed appreciation for my wonderful wife, Claudia, and enjoy spending time with my parents and brother. The best thing that has happened to me is meeting new friends along the way. My friends always seem available to help do whatever is necessary, and we have developed life-long relationships. If I am acting differently or am fatigued, they just accept me and go on with whatever we are doing.

Conclusion

LAURA'S THOUGHTS

Storms randomly enter our lives in varying degrees. Some are disturbing, but blow over. Others linger for a long period of time and change our lives forever. For believers, God never promised to take us out of the storm, but rather to give us a peace that passes all understanding in the storm. It would be much easier for us if He would smooth out the rough places in our lives and spare us the pain and heartache. However, He is more interested in how we approach the storm and come out on the other side. A storm of this proportion can provide a tremendous opportunity for growth in your personal walk with Him as you learn to lean heavily on your faith—or this can be a time of total devastation as you try to handle it alone in your own humanness. Twelve months after his brain injury, Bruce said, "This has been the best year of my life." He endured much difficulty and pain, but God brought us through with such spiritual growth that it was, indeed, the best year of our lives!

Don't look back and dwell on the past. Do what you can with what you have, and develop new ways of doing things. Remember: worry looks around, sorry looks back, and faith looks up. God has been faithful in so many ways throughout our life together and has shown that "He is our refuge and strength, always ready to help in times of trouble" (Psalm 46:1). We can do nothing except praise Him in the good times and the bad.

With some surgeries, you can be in and out of the hospital in a day or a week. Why does a brain injury take so long? The brain is the most complex machine in the world. Fixing it is not easy, but through its own plasticity, the brain can correct itself in many ways. The good news is that people *do* get better. It takes time—and a lot of faith—to get through to the other side of the storm, but you will get there.

BRUCE'S THOUGHTS

I wish I could say that everything is back to normal and that there are no aches or pains. I wish I could say I was back to work fulltime. Or do I? In fact, I really don't have time to go back to work. I'm so busy working with brain injury survivors that my days are full. Laura says that God is paying me through Social Security Disability so I can work totally for Him. He's a great boss, and the benefits are out of this world!

Sundays I sing in the choir at church. Being a pastor before, I never was able to sing in the choir. I love it. Music is wonderful therapy that helps rebuild my word bank. Mondays I recuperate from the weekend—rest is so important. Tuesdays I spend at MUST Ministries, where I give out bread goods to hundreds of people who need groceries, and attend the brain injury support group gathering. Wednesdays I do my "Honey Do List" and go to choir practice. Thursdays I visit various people God has brought my way and meet with a Bible Study group of fourteen people in the evening. Friday mornings is the fun breakfast where we talk about our adaptive skills and learn from each other. This is the highlight of my week. In my free time, I work out at the gym. On Saturdays Laura and I lead the family support group at Shepherd Center. Those that attend are usually in shock about what has happened to their family. It is an enriching time for us, and hopefully a helpful time for them.

In our free time (what little we have), we do fun things like go to the mountains, apple festivals, and the park to walk Princess. Rachel and I went rafting down the Chattahoochee River this summer on a double raft. That was exciting! I'm amazed at how God is using her testimony of our story to encourage the patients with whom she works at Shepherd Center.

If I could encourage you with one thought, I would say live in the present. I've heard it said that "the past is history, tomorrow is a mystery, but today well lived is a gift. That's why we call it the present!" My admonition to you is to live each moment to the fullest. That may mean taking a nap and giving your body a rest. Don't get too far ahead of yourself worrying about the future. Most of the things we worry about never come to pass, anyway—worry doesn't change anything.

I live by faith, and faith says, "This is the day the Lord has made. We will rejoice and be glad in it"(Psalm 118:24). "Faith is the confidence that what we hope for will actually happen; it gives us assurance about things we cannot see"(Hebrews 11:1). That means live in the present. Let tomorrow's worries take care of themselves. Even Jesus said, "Look at the lilies and how they grow. They don't work or make their clothing, yet Solomon in all his glory was not dressed as beautifully as they are"(Luke 12:27).

One of the great joys of my life, after I finished my rehab at Pathways and got involved in some small groups, was to marry off my two children! I actually performed both of the ceremonies. Our son, Jason, and his wife, Joanna, live in San Francisco, California, where they both practice law. Of course, he says the West Coast is the best coast. Being a lifelong Georgia boy, I'm not so sure about that.

It was also a thrill to walk Rachel down the aisle, and then perform her wedding this year. She has been such a blessing to us during my whole recovery process. At her wedding, I made the statement that she had not only been a wonderful daughter and a wonderful nurse, but had also become my best friend (besides Laura, of course).

My brother and my dad both ride road bicycles as I did prior to my surgery. I no longer ride the bike because of my balance issues. Dr. Kaelin also said a second head injury would not be as kind to me in recovery as this one has been. So, I stay off the bike. Whether you ride a bike, walk with a cane, or use a walker, celebrate each day for what it is. Minimize the difficulties and maximize the good along the journey.

Your life may have been touched by some catastrophic, life-changing event. Or perhaps you read this book to see what can happen to people and how they handle the struggles that come their way. We pray this time together has brought hope, encouragement, and information that will help you as you and others you know face the traumatic moments of life. God has a plan and purpose for each of us. He can take your mess, add some age, and turn it into a message to help others.

Trust in the Lord with all your heart; do not depend on your own understanding.
Seek his will in all you do, and he will
show you which path to take.
Proverbs 3:5–6

Mr. and Mrs. Jason Allen—May 24, 2009

Mr. and Mrs. Matthew Curry—May 21, 2011

About the Authors

Bruce Allen has been a pastor, writer, evangelist, and national senior consultant with John Maxwell's Injoy Stewardship Services before his brain injury. He holds a Bachelor of Arts in Journalism degree from the University of Georgia, a Master of Divinity, and a Doctor of Ministry from the Southern Baptist Theological Seminary, Louisville, Kentucky. Bruce devotes his time to ministering with brain injury survivors.

    Laura Fry Allen has been a speaker, writer, missionary, pastor's wife, and the National Evangelism Consultant with Women for the Southern Baptist North American Mission Board. She graduated from Southern Illinois University with a Bachelor of Arts degree in English, and a Master of Religious Education with emphasis in social work from Golden Gate Baptist Theological Seminary, Mill Valley, California. She currently works at Kennesaw State University in the WellStar School of Nursing.

    The Allens have been married thirty-one years and live in Marietta, Georgia, with their dog, Princess.

Laura and Bruce Allen

Appendix A

Glossary of People You May Meet

Laura Allen

Case Manager: A nurse experienced with brain injuries generally serves as the case manager who works as an advisor to the insurance company. The case manager will record the patient's lengthy medical history and be the advocate for the patient with the insurance company.

Dietitian: Due to a decrease in activity, a brain injury survivor may not be as physically active as before and, therefore, may gain weight. The dietitian will help in planning a healthier diet.

Ear, Nose, and Throat Doctor (ENT): A car accident may result in a broken nose or may difficulty in breathing. Sinus infections may happen repeatedly. This may result in needing to see an ENT.

Internal Medicine: This doctor "deals with the complex interactions of systems inside your body. The internist is usually a consultant rather than someone who follows your care from start to finish."[9]

---

[9]   Dr. Glen Johnson, *Traumatic Brain Injury Survival Guide,* June 25, 2010, http://www.tbiguide.com.

Neurologist: A neurologist who focuses on the brain and nerves deals with headaches and seizures by sometimes giving an EEG test or prescribes anti-seizure medication.

Neuropsychologist: A neuropsychologist is a psychologist with a specialty focus on how behavior is affected by brain injuries. This doctor may develop brain improvement strategies as well as counsel the patient and family through the recovery process.

Neurosurgeon: This surgeon performs surgeries related to the brain or nerves. The doctor tends to actually perform the surgery and then refer the patient to another long-term care doctor.

Nurses: Nurses are the medical caregivers for the brain injury survivor on a daily basis whether in the hospital, rehab center, or at home. They give out medications and carry out medical orders.

Occupational Therapist (OT): An OT works with the patient on skills needed in daily living. Another focus is high-level thinking skills necessary to return to life outside the rehab center.

Ophthalmologist (also called a neuro-ophthalmologist): An ophthalmologist is an eye doctor. Vision can change after an accident by becoming blurred, doubled, or exhibiting blank areas. The neuro-ophthalmologist specializes in vision problems caused by a brain injury.

Physical Therapist (PT): The physical ability to walk and move is the goal of the physical therapist. It takes much effort on the patient's part and may take a long time. The PT works with the patient to increase the range of motion for the legs, arms, and neck.

Plastic Surgeon: Plastic surgeons are specialists in removing scars. The surgery may be put off for six to nine months after the accident to give the scar tissue time to settle. Some scars are basically invisible after this type of treatment.

Psychiatrist: Emotional or behavioral problems are the specialties of a psychiatrist. Medication is often prescribed to deal with intense behavior, emotions, or depression.

Psychologist: Psychologists do not prescribe medications. They work closely with coping and behavioral skills. Often standardized tests are administered to measure various aptitudes and the recovery process.

Radiologist: A radiologist diagnoses problems by using imaging equipment such as X-rays, CT Scans, or MRIs, and then reports the results to the physician.

Recreational Therapist (RT): A recreational therapist focuses on the fun things of life. The RT will explore the patient's interests, skills, and hobbies to see what old and new recreational skills can be developed or adapted to this new way of life.

Speech/Language Pathologist (also called a speech therapist or ST): Improving a patient's speech patterns and cognitive problems are the focuses of a speech therapist. Attention, memory, organization, planning, sequencing, writing skills and reading comprehension are also involved in the work of a speech therapist.

Dr. Chris Hagen, Danese Malkmus, and Patricia Durham

Appendix B

Family Guide to the Rancho Levels of Cognitive Functioning

Cognition refers to a person's thinking and memory skills. Cognitive skills include paying attention, being aware of one's surroundings, organizing, planning, following through on decisions, solving problems, judgment, reasoning, and awareness of problems. Memory skills include the ability to remember things before and after the brain injury. Because of the damage caused by a brain injury, some or all of these skills will be changed.

The Rancho Levels of Cognitive Functioning is an evaluation tool used by the rehabilitation team. The eight levels describe the patterns or stages of recovery typically seen after a brain injury. This helps the team understand and focus on the person's abilities and design an appropriate treatment program. Each person will progress at their own rate, depending on the severity of the brain damage, the location of the injury in the brain and length of time since the brain injury. Some individuals will pass through each of the eight levels, while others may progress to a certain level and fail to change to the next higher level.

It is important to remember that each person is an individual and there are many factors that need to be considered when assigning a level of cognition. There are a range of abilities within each of the levels and your family member may exhibit some or all of the behaviors listed below.

COGNITIVE LEVEL I
NO RESPONSE
A person at this level will or may:
- Be unresponsive to sounds, sights, touch or movement.

COGNITIVE LEVEL II
GENERALIZED RESPONSE
A person at this level will or may:
- Begin to respond to sounds, sights, touch or movement
- Respond slowly, inconsistently, or after a delay
- Respond in the same way to what they hear, see or feel; responses may include chewing, sweating, breathing faster, moaning, moving, and increasing blood pressure

COGNITIVE LEVEL III
LOCALIZED RESPONSE
A person at this level will or may:
- Be awake on and off during the day
- Make more movements than before; react more specifically to what they see, hear, or feel. For example, they may turn towards a sound, withdraw from pain, and attempt to watch a person move around the room
- React slowly and inconsistently
- Begin to recognize family and friends

- Follow some simple directions such as "look at me" or "squeeze my hand"
- Begin to respond inconsistently to simple questions with "yes" and "no" head nods
- Respond more consistently to familiar people.

What family/friends can do at Cognitive Levels I, II, and III:

- Keep the room calm and quiet.
- Keep comments and questions short and simple.
- Explain what is about to be done using a "calm" tone of voice.
- Limit the number of visitors to two to three people at a time.
- Allow the person extra time to respond, but don't expect responses to be correct.
- Give the person rest periods.
- Tell the person who you are, where they are, why they are in the hospital, and what day it is.
- Bring in favorite belongings and pictures of family members.
- Engage the person in familiar activities, such as listening to their favorite music, talking about their family and friends, reading out loud to the person, watching TV, combing their hair, putting on lotion, etc.

COGNITIVE LEVEL IV
CONFUSED AND AGITATED
A person at this level will or may:

- Be very confused and frightened
- Not understand what they feel or what is happening around them
- Overreact to what they see, hear, or feel by hitting, screaming, using abusive language, or thrashing

about. In some cases, they may need to be restrained to prevent hurting themselves or others
- Be highly focused on their basic needs; i.e. eating, relieving pain, going back to bed, going to the bathroom, or going home
- May not understand that people are trying to help them
- Not pay attention or be unable to concentrate for more than a few seconds
- Have difficulty following directions
- Recognize family/friends some of the time; with help, be able to do simple routine activities as feeding themselves, dressing or talking.

What family/friends can do at Cognitive Level IV:
- Allow the person as much movement as is safe.
- Allow the person to choose activities, and follow their lead, within safety limits. Do not force the person to do tasks or activities.
- Give the person breaks and change activities frequently especially if they are easily distracted, restless or agitated.
- Keep the room quiet and calm. For example, turn off the TV and radio, don't talk too much and use a calm voice.
- Limit the number of visitors to two or three people at a time.
- Experiment to find familiar activities that are calming to the person such as listening to music, eating, etc.
- Bring in family pictures and personal items from home, to make the person feel more comfortable.
- Tell the person where they are and reassure the person that they are safe.

- Take the person for rides, if the person uses a wheelchair. If ambulatory, take the person for short walks in a safe environment.

COGNITIVE LEVEL V
CONFUSED, INAPPROPRIATE, NONAGITATED
A person at this level will or may:
- Be able to pay attention for only a few minutes
- Be confused and have difficulty making sense of things around them
- Not know the date, where they are or why they are in the hospital
- Need step-by-step instructions to start or complete everyday activities, such as brushing their teeth, even when physically able
- Become overwhelmed and restless when tired or when there are too many people around
- Have a poor memory. They will remember past events which happened prior to the accident better than their daily routine or information they have been told since the injury
- Try to fill in gaps in memory by making things up
- May get stuck on an idea or activity and need help switching to the next step
- Focus on basic needs such as eating, relieving pain, going back to bed, going to the bathroom, or going home.

What family/friends can do at Cognitive Level V:
- Repeat questions or comments as needed. Don't assume they will remember what you have told the person previously.
- Tell the person the day, date, name and location of the hospital, and why they are in the hospital when you first arrive and before you leave.

- Keep a calendar and list of visitors available.
- Keep comments and questions short and simple.
- Help the person organize and get started on an activity.
- Limit the number of visitors to two or three people at a time.
- Give the person frequent rest periods when they have problems paying attention.
- Limit the number of questions you ask. Try not to "test" the patient by asking a lot of questions.
- Help the person connect what they remember with what is currently going on with their family, friends and favorite activities.
- Bring in family pictures and personal items from home.
- Reminisce about familiar and fun past activities.

COGNITIVE LEVEL VI
CONFUSED AND APPROPRIATE
A person at this level will or may:
- Be somewhat confused because of memory and thinking problems. Will remember main points from a conversation, but forget and confuse the details; for example, they may remember they had visitors in the morning, but forget what they talked about
- Follow a schedule with some help, but become confused by changes in the routine
- Know the month and year, unless there is a severe memory problem
- Pay attention for about 30 minutes, but have trouble concentrating when it is noisy or when the activity involves many steps. For example, at an intersection, they may not be able to step off the curb, watch for cars, watch the traffic light, walk, and talk at the same time

- Brush their teeth, get dressed, feed themselves etc., with help; know when they need to use the bathroom
- Do or say things too fast, without thinking about potential consequences
- Know that they are hospitalized because of an injury, but will not understand all of the problems they are having
- Be more aware of physical problems than thinking problems. They often associate their problems with being in the hospital and think they'll be fine at home.

What family/friends can do at Cognitive Level VI:
- Repeat things. Discuss things that have happened during the day to help the person improve their ability to recall what they have been doing and learning.
- Encourage the person to repeat information that they need or want to remember.
- Provide cues to help the person start and continue activities.
- Encourage the person to use familiar visual and written information to help the person with their memory (e.g. calendar).
- Encourage the person to participate in all therapies. They will not fully understand the extent of their problems and the benefits of therapy.
- Encourage the person to write down something about what they have done each day.

COGNITIVE LEVEL VII
AUTOMATIC AND APPROPRIATE
A person at this level will or may:
- Follow a set schedule
- Be able to do routine self-care without help, if physically able. For example, they can dress or feed themselves independently

- Have problems in new situations and may become frustrated or act without thinking first
- Have problems planning, starting, and following through with activities;
- Have trouble paying attention in distracting or stressful situations. For example, family gatherings, work, school, church, or sports events
- Not realize how their thinking and memory problems may affect future plans and goals; therefore, they may expect to quickly return to their previous lifestyle or work
- Continue to need supervision because of decreased safety awareness and judgment. They still do not fully understand the impact of their physical or thinking problems
- Think more slowly in stressful situations; be inflexible or rigid, and they may seem stubborn. These behaviors are common after brain injury
- Be able to talk about doing something, but will have problems actually doing it.

COGNITIVE LEVEL VIII
PURPOSEFUL AND APPROPRIATE
A person at this level will or may:
- Realize that they have a problems with their thinking and memory skills
- Begin to compensate for their problems; be more flexible and less rigid in their thinking; for example, they may be able to come up with more than one way to solve a problem
- Be ready for driving or job training evaluation
- Be able to learn new things at a slower rate
- Still become overwhelmed in difficult, stressful, rapidly changing or emergency situations

- Show poor judgment in new situations and may require assistance
- Need some guidance to make decisions
- Have thinking problems that may not be noticeable to people who did not know the person before the injury

What family/friends can do at Cognitive Levels VII/VIII:
- Treat the person as an adult while still providing guidance and assistance in decision making. Their opinions should be respected and their feelings should be validated.
- Talk with the person as an adult. Use a natural and respectful tone of voice and attitude. You may need to limit the amount of information or the complexity of the vocabulary, but do not talk down to the person.
- Be careful when joking or using slang, because the person may take things literally and misunderstand the meaning. Also, be careful about teasing the person.
- Be sure to check with the physicians on the person's restrictions concerning driving, working, and other activities. Do not rely only on the person with the brain injury for information, since they may feel they are ready to go back to their previous lifestyle right away.
- Help the person participate in family activities. As the person begins to see some of the problems they have in thinking, problem solving, and memory, talk with the person about how to deal with these problems without criticizing the person. Reassure the person that the problems are caused by the brain injury.
- Strongly encourage the person to continue with therapy to increase their thinking, memory and physical abilities. They may feel that they are completely

normal. However, they are still making progress and may benefit from continued treatment.

- Discourage the person from drinking or using drugs, due to medical complications. If substance abuse is an issue, encourage the person to seek outside help.
- Encourage the person to use note taking as a way to help with their remaining learning problems.
- Encourage the person to do their self-care and other daily activities as independently as possible.
- Discuss what kinds of situations make the person angry and what they can do in these situations.
- Talk with the person about their feelings.
- Help the person think about what they are going to do before they do it, and practice before they actually do it. Afterward, talk about how it went and what might work better next time.
- Consult with Social Work and Psychology. Learning to live with a brain injury is difficult. It may take a long time for the person and family to adjust.

For further information, please call Rancho at 1-877-RANCHO-1 or visit www.rancho.org

Appendix C

Care for the Caregiver

Jean Kropa, Caregiver, M. Ed., CCC, SLP

The one area that I would like to emphasize with you is **caring for yourself.** Now is a good time for you to "give yourself extra attention."

Others in your family are taking care of the house, food, minor crises, etc. It is a learning time for them; when you return home, they will be able to do continue some of the work, giving you time for other more complex things. The chronic stress of doing everything for everybody can be wearing on the body; *delegation,* when it is possible, can be a very good thing. When you get your patient back home, it will be more important; their help will allow you to be more focused on providing care and guidance as recovery continues.

Some ways that I have used to focus on myself are an occasional manicure, a "shampoo and set", and a hot, soaking bath (followed by a self-massage of my feet in hot water, then with a fragrant body lotion). Sometimes I sip a cup of tea, and watch some birds, squirrels, and chipmunks, or go to a quiet place and watch the setting sun. Other times I will close my eyes and remember a relaxing vacation place.

Visualizing what makes me relax, or what I would like to happen, can be calming and inspirational. I like to "see" myself in a cool, mountain valley...in late spring...listening to birds and a waterfall...as I lie on the soft grass...looking at the new flowers and towering, surrounding mountains...as I lie under a large shade tree and no one else is there. The "journey" to get from where I am to there and then back to where I am, is a progressively relaxing process. (Some like to "go" to a beach and "hear" the waves slapping on the shore—I am sensitive to the sun, though, so that doesn't work for me.)

Taking care of yourself also includes getting enough food, exercise, and sunlight (this can be a trick when you "live" at the hospital), and enough good sleep. Stress is a chronic condition at a hospital, so your positive attitude with your sense of humor (laughing is very good for you) are important to maintain.

It is okay for your TBI survivor to have some time without you at the bedside; it is also okay for them to acknowledge that you are not able to make every wish miraculously happen. They will have to do much of the regaining and learning of skills by persistence and hard work. You know that they are able to do that; you can provide some motivation and encouragement to keep on trying until they stop getting better.

Try to be patient with the patient. Their thoughts, words, and actions have gotten scrambled; they will sound confused; they do not realize their current limitations. Give them extra time for everything. They usually cannot remember new, short-term memory entries into their brains. Answer the same question a dozen times. They want to be better as much as you want them to be better.

Appendix D

Top Ten Tips for Caregivers

From American Heart Association

The National Family Caregivers Association offers these ten tips for family caregivers:

1. Choose to take charge of your life, and don't let your loved one's illness or disability always take center stage.

2. Remember to be good to yourself. Love, honor and value yourself. You're doing a very hard job, and you deserve some quality time just for you.

3. Watch for signs of depression and don't delay in getting professional help when you need it.

4. When people offer to help, accept the offer and suggest specific things they can do.

5. Educate yourself about your loved one's condition. Information is empowering.

6. There's a difference between caring and doing. Be open to new technologies and ideas that promote your loved one's independence and help you do your job easier.

7. Trust your instincts. Most of the time they'll lead you in the right direction.

8. Grieve for your losses, and then allow yourself to dream new dreams.

9. Stand up for your rights as a caregiver and as a citizen.

10. Seek support from other caregivers. There is great strength in knowing that you are not alone.

TOP TEN TIPS TO REFRESH YOURSELF

Time out is essential, not only for peace and quiet, but to get things done for your life. If you try to wait for all of your chores and responsibilities to your loved one to be finished, you may be waiting a long time. **Get started now to find time to refresh yourself.**

Here's a list of the top ten things you need to do regularly:

1. **Get regular physical activity.** Regular, moderate-to-vigorous physical activity is a good energizer that reduces stress, helps keep blood pressure and cholesterol at heart-healthy levels and helps maintain a healthy weight. Aim for thirty minutes a day on most, if not all, days. You can break it down to ten- or fifteen-minute sessions. Walking is a great way to get started, even if you only walk around the yard.

2. **Eat heart-healthy foods.** They give you more energy, keep your brain fed (which helps combat depression) and help prevent other health problems. If you've got to "eat on the run," choose nutritious snacks.

3. **Take time every day for an activity that you enjoy** such as reading, listening to music, crafts, cooking — whatever makes you happy and relaxes you.

4. **Keep humor in your life.** Laughter *is* good medicine. Find the humor in your situation when possible, watch a silly TV program, or pop in a comedy movie. Find things to laugh about with your loved one. They need joy, too! Laughing quickens the pulse rate, stimulates the blood circulation, activates muscles, increases oxygen intake, and helps you relax. If you've forgotten how to laugh, try to be around people who still know how. Laughter's contagious!

5. **Get out once a week and go somewhere enjoyable.** Visit the local coffee shop, attend church events, take a class, visit a friend, or just wander around the mall or a park. If your loved one needs constant attention, ask for help. You can find someone to give an hour a week to let you get out.

6. **Treat depression and stress.** Recognize signs and symptoms and do something about it as soon as it starts. If you think you may be depressed, get professional help. Talk it out. Admit your feelings.

7. **Take care of your business.** Keep your checkbook balanced, work when you need to, spend time with friends and family, and don't stop planning for the future. It's out there waiting for you. If you live totally "in the moment" of your caregiver responsibilities, you'll find it more difficult to re-integrate into life later on. Keep living.

8. **Keep all your medical and dental appointments.** Do all you can to keep from getting sick. If you're sick, you won't be able to do what your loved one

needs. Ask for help when you need it to get away and take care of your health.

9. **Think positive**. Take time every day to refresh your mind. Admit your limitations. Let go of guilt. Admit that you're angry. Pat yourself on the back for the job you're doing. If you're feeling guilty or angry, take a break.

10. **Stay connected with the outside world**, even if it's just by phone or online. Don't isolate yourself. Talk to friends about something other than your situation. Stay interested in what would be going on in your life if you weren't caregiving. It's still there and you're still a part of it.

Did you know? Medical studies show that laughter boosts levels of endorphins, the body's "feel-good" hormones. Laughter may even boost the immune system. A good attitude and exercising your sense of humor may reduce stress, lower depression, and help your body and mind to heal. As Groucho Marx said, "A clown is like an aspirin, only he works twice as fast."

Appendix E

Anger, Frustration and Anxiety: A Day in the Life of the Brain Injured

Stuart Hanzman, LCSW
stuarthanzman@aol.com

Acquired Brain Injury (ABI) occurs when a person has experienced an injury to the brain that results from an accident or illness. This may include a traumatic brain injury from a motor vehicle or work related accident or a tumor, stroke and other related illnesses. The damage can cause temporary or permanent deficits depending on the severity of the trauma and where on the brain it occurred.

Problems can occur, such as in speech, vision, strength, coordination, cognition and memory, limb weakness or hemi paresis, and other physical impairments in addition to behavioral and emotional disorders.

Persons with an ABI often experience labile (rapidly changing) mood and behaviors as a result of the physiological and emotional manifestations of the injury. This can be caused by the damage to related areas of the brain, such as frontal lobe injury which regulates behaviors and emotions. Adjustment problems are very common due to the devastating changes in employment, social and family relationships, thinking, strength, stamina, etc.

Emotional responses may include but are not limited to, anger, frustration, anxiety, depression, poor coping, fear, disbelief, outbursts, rage, impulsivity, paranoia, withdrawal, low self-esteem, and lack of confidence.

These emotions are fluid, often irrational and can arise without provocation (seemingly). The brain injured person may quickly become angry, sad or frustrated and have difficulty explaining the causes. Often, the ABI individual speaks of feeling isolated and poorly understood. This is more prominent when they have little physical impairments to call attention to their brain injury, resulting in a lack of empathy from others.

Brain injury is the most mysterious and least understood of all major illnesses. People too often think the person is mentally ill, under the influence of alcohol or drugs, malingering or just not able to "move on" past the trauma.

Persons with ABI often wonder why they feel good one minute and so miserable the next. How can their memory function so well in the morning and so poorly in the evening, or when stressed, sick, or over stimulated? Why can't they perform the tasks they did every day before the accident or illness? Why is everyone so unsupportive about brain injury?

A common question asked by the inflicted person is what causes these rapid and unexplained changes and how can they be controlled. Too often, medical personnel are unable to provide concrete solutions for their concerns and often answer with "I don't know" to the many questions asked. Moodiness, angry outbursts, agitation and inappropriate behaviors often results, keeping them further isolated.

Family members also have a poor understanding of the manifestations from an ABI. They too are frustrated, scared, and overwhelmed by the multiple changes in cognition, emotions and physical stamina. The spouse has to become the primary breadwinner and caregiver, losing a partner and confidant. The children are also intimidated by the changes in their parent, often reversing roles with the former adult figure. The family members are frightened by the anger, confused about the new personality, and worried about their bleak future and financial status.

Family members often ask:

- If you look so good, why are you not healed?
- What can't you go back to work, school, and your normal routine? Why are you always so angry, worried, or sad?
- Why do you remember some things but not others?
- Why do you sleep so much?

The only consistent element of an ABI is the inconsistency of the symptoms. It is common for a person with a brain injury to feel refreshed, vibrant, and enthusiastic in the morning, and completely drained by noon, unable to perform even the simplest of tasks. Family members, friends, and employers do not understand how a person can "swing" so quickly and become dysfunctional and irritable in an instant, requiring naps and extended sleep.

Brain injured persons are hyper-sensitive to fatigue, stimulation, stress, physical illness and other events that would not disable a fully functional person. This causes further confusion about an already poorly understood disease process (ABI) that affects the entire body system. They have no cognitive and physical reserve to draw from, exacerbating their impairments. When stressed, the injured person may also exhibit disinhibition: acting out thoughts without awareness of how their actions affect others, such as yelling, cursing, or other inappropriate behaviors.

As with other diseases, this is no cure for an acquired brain injury. Medications, exercise, balance between rest and activity, therapies, utilization of compensatory strategies, reduced stimulation, positive coping, counseling, support groups, family support, and acceptance all help to heal the brain and allow it to develop new pathways for learning. New research also suggests the brain can develop new cells over time.

When the brain injured person is first ill or injured, often near death, there is an outpouring of support from family, friends and co-workers. Once they recover from the initial trauma, the family is so grateful that they have survived they do not think about the long term consequences such as finances, changes in behavior, twenty-four hour supervision and activities of daily living.

Months later, supervisors whom were initially very comforting about job security and benefits quickly retreat behind human resources. The family is left destitute, abandoned, and overwhelmed. Friends and family are too busy to help, employers don't return phone calls, and Social Security requests multiple documentations for the fifth time. The brain injury patient feels rejected and frustrated, unable to cope or ask for help. They become depressed and helpless about their lives and the future. The see little opportunity for improvement and may become paranoid, withdrawing into confusion and isolation.

Due to the behavioral and emotional liability, people become fearful or annoyed by the impulsive outbursts. The brain's normal filters and mechanisms for self-control have been damaged. The injured person has lost their problem solving abilities, resulting in racing thoughts and bizarre behavior. Without a strong support system, they may become hostile, defiant or suicidal.

What should professionals and family members do to help the brain injured person?

- Provide unconditional support and understanding of the brain injury
- Stay calm; acknowledge that the behaviors are from the brain injury

- Encourage rest and relaxation, especially when they are stressed or upset
- Encourage stress reduction activities (deep breathing, walks, counting, and music)
- Monitor medications, as appropriate with frequent re-evaluation as needed for behavior/mood
- Work closely with a physiatrist (physical medicine and rehab physician)
- Encourage exercise (cleared by the physician)
- Encourage therapies (physical, occupational, speech/cognitive, vocational)
- Consume balanced nutrition; avoid sugar and caffeine
- Eat three meals a day; eat by the clock, not by hunger alone (avoid drop in blood sugar)
- Attend individual and family counseling
- Attend support groups
- Maintain realistic expectation
- Don't overreact to the behaviors or emotions
- Take one day at a time

Lastly, research show that persons with a brain injury who receives good support heal quicker, have fewer behavioral and emotional problems and adjust better than those that do not. Counseling and support groups are great resources for brain injury.

For more information and a list of statewide brain injury support groups, visit the Brain Injury Association of Georgia's website at www.braininjurygeorgia.org, call 404-712-5504, or email info@braininjurygeorgia.org.

Reprinted with Permission
©2007 Stuart Hanzman, LCSW

Appendix F

Traumatic Brain Injury Facts Understanding Brain Injury

From Centers for Disease Control and Prevention

What should you know about brain injury and recovery? Go to www.braininjury101.org to watch a series of incredible videos produced by the Shepherd Center. These videos feature some of the nation's top physicians, neuroscientists, and brain injury experts to help you understand brain injury and give you practical advice for coping with brain injury.

- 1.7 million Americans sustain a traumatic brain injury each year. Approximately 475,000 of these cases are children[10]
- Georgia averages 57,000+ traumatic brain injuries each year with 20,000+ Georgia children either treated in an emergency department or hospitalized.
- The leading causes of traumatic brain injury in Georgia are falls (49.88%), motor vehicle crashes

---

[10] Mark Faul, Likang Xu, Marlena M. Wald, and Victor G. Coronado, *Traumatic Brain Injury in the United States: Emergency Department Visits, Hospitalizations, and Deaths* (Atlanta, GA: Centers for Disease Control and Prevention, 2010).

(24.36%), being struck by an object or person (14.3%), and violence (11.4%).

- People with traumatic brain injury are at a higher risk for psychiatric disorders.
- The prevalence of depression in the general population is around 5%, while the prevalence of depression in head trauma patients can reach an astounding 40%.
- Professional sports programs like the National Football League have been leading efforts to prevent concussions sustained on the field. These and other prevention initiatives have followed claims that numerous cases of depression and suicide, such as that of Philadelphia Eagles player Andre Waters in November 2006, are linked to a series of concussions.[11]

GET THE STATS ON TRAUMATIC BRAIN INJURY IN THE UNITED STATES

Each year, traumatic brain injuries (TBI) contribute to a substantial number of deaths and cases of permanent disability. A TBI is caused by a bump, blow or jolt to the head or a penetrating head injury that disrupts the normal function of the brain. The severity of a TBI may range from "mild" to "severe".

Data are critical to understanding the impact of this important public health problem. This information can help inform TBI prevention strategies, identify research and education priorities, and support the need for services among those living with a TBI.

---

[11] *Brain Injury Peer Visitor Association.* 2011. http://www.braininjurypeervisitor.org.

ESTIMATED AVERAGE ANNUAL NUMBER OF TBI IN THE UNITED STATES 2002-2006

TBI in the United States

- An estimated 1.7 million people sustain a TBI annually. Of them:
- 52,000 die
- 275,000 are hospitalized
- 1.365 million, nearly 80%, are treated and released from an emergency department.
- TBI is a contributing factor to a third (30.5%) of all injury-related deaths in the United States.
- About 75% of TBIs that occur each year are concussions or other forms of mild traumatic brain injury.
- Direct medical costs and indirect costs of TBI, such as lost productivity, totaled an estimated $60 billion in the United States in 2000.

TBI by Age

- Children aged 0 to 4 years, older adolescents aged 15 to 19 years, and adults aged 65 years and older are most likely to sustain a TBI.
- Almost half a million (473,947) emergency department visits for TBI are made annually by children aged 0 to 14 years.
- Adults aged 75 years and older have the highest rates of TBI-related hospitalization and death.

TBI by Sex
- In every age group, TBI rates are higher for males than for females.
- Males aged 0 to 4 years have the highest rates of TBI-related emergency department visits, hospitalizations, and deaths combined.

TBI by External Cause
- Falls are the leading cause of TBI. Rates are highest for children aged 0 to 4 years and for adults aged 75 years and older.
- Falls result in the greatest number of TBI-related emergency department visits (523,043) and hospitalizations (62,334).
- Motor vehicle–traffic injury is the leading cause of TBI-related death. Rates are highest for adults aged 20 to 24 years.

Additional TBI Findings
- There was an increase in TBI-related emergency department visits (14.4%) and hospitalizations (19.5%) from 2002 to 2006.
- There was a 62% increase in fall-related TBI seen in emergency departments among children aged 14 years and younger from 2002 to 2006.
- There was an increase in fall-related TBI among adults aged 65 and older; 46% increase in emergency department visits, 34% increase in hospitalizations, and 27% increase in TBI-related deaths from 2002 to 2006.[12]

CDC analyzed existing national data sets for its report, *Traumatic Brain Injury in the United States: Emergency Department*

---

[12] Dr. Eric Finkelstein, Dr. Phaedra Corso, and Dr. Ted Miller, *The Incidence and Economic Burden of Injuries in the United States,* (New York: Oxford University Press, 2006).

Visits, Hospitalizations and Deaths 2002–2006. CDC's National Center for Injury Prevention and Control funds 30 states to conduct TBI surveillance through the CORE State Injury Program. TBI-related death and hospitalization data submitted by participating CORE states are published in CDC's *State Injury Indicators Report.*[13]

---

[13] *Report to Congress on Mild Traumatic Brain Injury in the United States: Steps to Prevent a Serious Public Health Problem* (Atlanta, GA: Centers for Disease Control and Prevention, 2003).

Appendix G

Glasgow Coma Scale

From Centers for Disease Control and Prevention

Eye Opening Response
- Spontaneous--open with blinking at baseline **4 points**
- To verbal stimuli, command, speech **3 points**
- To pain only (not applied to face) **2 points**
- No response **1 point**

Verbal Response
- Oriented **5 points**
- Confused conversation, but able to answer questions **4 points**
- Inappropriate words **3 points**
- Incomprehensible speech **2 points**
- No response **1 point**

Motor Response
- Obeys commands for movement **6 points**
- Purposeful movement to painful stimulus **5 points**
- Withdraws in response to pain **4 points**

- Flexion in response to pain (decorticate posturing) **3 points**
- Extension response in response to pain (decerebrate posturing) **2 points**
- No response **1 point**

Categorization: Coma: No eye opening, no ability to follow commands, no word verbalizations (3-8)

Head Injury Classification: Severe Head Injury—GCS score of 8 or less Moderate Head Injury—GCS score of 9 to 12 Mild Head Injury—GCS score of 13 to 15 (Adapted from: Advanced Trauma Life Support: Course for Physicians, American College of Surgeons, 1993).

Disclaimer: Based on motor responsiveness, verbal performance, and eye opening to appropriate stimuli, the Glasgow Coma Scale was designed and should be used to assess the depth and duration of coma and impaired consciousness. This scale helps to gauge the impact of a wide variety of conditions such as acute brain damage due to traumatic and/or vascular injuries or infections, metabolic disorders (e.g., hepatic or renal failure, hypoglycemia, diabetic ketosis), etc.

Resources

Suggested Reading

- **Brain Injury Medicine: Principles and Practice**
  Nathan D. Zasler, Douglas I. Katz, and Ross D.
  Zafonte. New York: Demos Medical Publishing LLC;
  2007.

  A comprehensive guide to all aspects of the
  management issues involved in caring for the
  person with brain injury—from early diagnosis
  and evaluation through the post-acute period and
  rehabilitation.

- **Brain Injury Survival Kit, 365 Tips, Tools, and
  Tricks to Deal with Cognitive Loss**
  Cheryle Sullivan. New York: Demos Medical
  Publishing LLC; 2008.

  Survivors of both minor and severe brain injuries
  will find this book to be an invaluable guide to
  overcoming the challenges they face every day.
  Written in a sparse easy-to-read manner, this book
  is ideal for teaching survivors (and their caregivers)
  how to use specific and concrete strategies

and assistive devices to address their impaired attention, memory, organization, communication, and other executive functioning skills.

- **Change Your Brain, Change Your Life: The Breakthrough Program for Conquering Anxiety, Depression, Obsessiveness, Anger, and Impulsiveness**
Daniel G. Amen, M.D. New York: Three Rivers Press; 1998.

  The book is engaging, informative, and most importantly, offers a great deal of hope.

- **Head Injury: The Facts: A Guide for Families and Care-givers**
Dorothy Gronwall, Phillip Wrightson, and Peter Waddell. England: Oxford University Press; 2002.

  This book is an excellent overview of the basic facts associated with brain injury. It clearly presents the nature of brain injury and the aftermath, both immediate and long term. It relates incidents of behavior and ways of coping with the difficulties during the recovery period.

- **Living With Brain Injury: A Guide for Families**
Richard Senelick, Cathy Ryan, and Karla Dougherty. Birmingham, Alabama: HealthSouth Press; 2010.

  The authors believe that there is life after brain injury. They provide a guide to help you accomplish this.

- **The Mild Traumatic Brain Injury Workbook**
Douglas J. Mason and Marc Sharfman. Oakland, California: New Harbinger Publications; 2004.

This very thorough book gives an overview of traumatic brain injury (TBI), then breaks TBI down into all of the individual problems associated with TBI such as the anatomy of the brain, what happens to the brain after TBI, measuring the severity, setting goals, medical care, physical aspects of TBI, how the senses are involved, cognitive issues, and emotions. Mental exercises—mazes, number and letter searches, abstract puzzles, etc.— are included throughout the book.

BOOKS BY SURVIVORS OF BRAIN INJURY

- **Coping With Mild Traumatic Brain Injury**
Diane Roberts Stoler and Barbara Albers Hill. New York: Penguin Putnam Inc.; 1998.

A brain injury survivor, Dr. Stoler covers every aspect of brain injury, such as how the brain works, how the brain can be injured, procedures used to diagnose and treat the brain, common physical, mental, and psychological symptoms of brain injury, suggestions for coping, advice on financial, insurance, family matters, the rehabilitation process and possible outcomes, etc.

- **Gabby: A Story of Courage and Hope**
Alison Hanson, Mark Kelly, Jeffrey Zaslow, and Gabrielle Giffords. New York: Scribner; 2011.

Gabby Giffords, a senator from Arizona, was shot in the head at a political rally in Tucson. This book is written primarily by her husband about her efforts over the past ten months to relearn how to walk and talk. This memoir offers a personal look at her slow, agonizing recovery from a brain injury.

- **In An Instant: A Family's Journey of Love and Healing**
Lee Woodruff and Bob Woodruff. New York: Random House, Inc.; 2007.

  This is the true story of how ABC News anchor Bob Woodruff sustained a brain injury in January 2006 while in Iraq, and how he and his family coped with his injury and recovery process. This is a frank, compelling, yet heartfelt account. Their story is told from both Lee's (his wife) and Bob's perspectives.

- **My Stroke of Insight: A Brain Scientist's Personal Journey**
Jill Bolte Taylor. England: Hodder & Stoughton; 2008.

  Jill's journey and thoughts are tremendously helpful! She gives much information and specifics of her experience from a brain scientist's vantage point.

- **Tour de Life: From Coma to Competition**
Saul Raisin and Dave Shields. Salt Lake City, UT: Three Story Press; 2007.

  The Raisin parents are two ordinary people who rise to an extraordinary challenge with brilliance. Saul is amazing in his fierce desire to get back to "normal."

Brain Injury Movies

- **Regarding Henry**
  Directed by Mike Nichols, with Harrison Ford, Annette Bening, and Michael Haley. Paramount Pictures, 1991.

  If we suffered a serious brain injury or a spinal cord break, would we survive and cope? This film shows one fictional man facing that crisis and becoming a better man for having lost some of his mental toughness and job skills from a TBI.

Brain Injury Links

- **How Aphasia Feels**
  www.Aphasiacorner.com/aphasia-simulations/

  The simulations show what it might be like to have this language disorder that affects more than one million people in the United States.

- **Understanding Brain Injury**
  www.braininjury101.org

  What should you know about brain injury and recovery? Watch a series of incredible videos produced by the Shepherd Center. The videos feature some of the nation's top physicians, neuroscientists, and brain injury experts to help you understand brain injury and give you practical advice for coping with brain injury.

- **The Brain & Spinal Injury Trust Fund Commission**
  www.bsitf.state.ga.us

  Georgians with traumatic brain and spinal injuries deserve lives of independence and inclusion—lives rich with vision and possibilities. Trust fund awards assist individuals with injuries in reaching these goals.

- **BrainLine**
  www.brainline.org

  BrainLine is a national multimedia project offering information and resources about preventing, treating, and living with a brain injury. It includes a series of webcasts, electronic newsletters, and an extensive outreach campaign in partnership with national organizations concerned about brain injury. There are twenty-four life-changing iPhone and iPad apps for people with brain injury covered on the website (Note: some are free, some have a fee).

- **CaringBridge**
  www.caringbridge.org

  CaringBridge offers free websites that support and connect family members and friends during critical illnesses, treatment, and recovery. This is an easy way to keep everyone up-to-date on your survivor's progress.

- **CDC—Heads Up: Concussion in Youth Sports**
  www.cdc.gov/concussioninYouthSports

  To help ensure the health and safety of young athletes, CDC developed the "Heads Up: Concussion in Youth Sports" initiative to offer information about concussions—a type of traumatic brain injury—to coaches, parents, and athletes involved in youth sports.

- **Centers for Medicare and Medicaid Services**
www.cms.hhs.gov

    This site offers extensive information about Medicare and Medicaid insurance programs.

- **Children's Brain Injury Association**
www.childrensbraininjury.org

    Started in 2010, Children's Brain Injury Association's mission is to provide support, funding, and assist with research for the treatment of children who have a brain injury. They serve children all across the United States.

- **Defense and Veterans Brain Injury Center**
www.dvbic.org

    The DVBIC serves active duty military, their dependents, and veterans with brain injury through state-of-the-art medical care, innovative clinical research initiatives, and educational programs. Information is available in Spanish.

- **disABILITY LINK**
www.disABILITYLINK.org

    The Center for Independent Living serving Metro Atlanta—a cross-disability, not-for-profit, grass-roots organization run by and for people with disabilities—supporting people with disabilities to be in charge of their own lives by having choices, making decisions, and taking responsibility for themselves.

- **Medical Resources: Traumatic Brain Injuries**
  www.medicalassistantdegree.com/resources/medical-resources-traumatic-brain-injuries

  A very good resource guide for people interested in brain injury.

- **Medicare**
  www.medicare.org

  Offers everything you need and want to know about Medicare and how it works. Provides information on how to enroll, what is covered, how to get additional insurance and connections to your state system.

- **Medline Plus**
  www.nlm.nih.gov/medlineplus/traumaticbraininjury.html
  www.nlm.nih.gov/medlineplus/caregivers.html

  Medline Plus is a service of the U.S. National Library of Medicine and the National Institutes of Health. The Medline Plus website provides authoritative information about brain injury and caregiving produced and compiled by U.S. government agencies and health-related organizations. The site also provides easy access to medical journal articles and has extensive information about drugs, an illustrated medical encyclopedia, interactive patient tutorials, and the latest health news.

- **Mothers Against Brain Injury**
  www.mabii.org

  One of the leading organizations dedicated to providing hope, comfort, and valuable information to families experiencing a traumatic brain injury with a loved one.

- **The National Aphasia Association**
  www.aphasia.org

  Lists resources, materials and support group information to help people with aphasia and their families.

- **The National Brain Injury Association**
  www.biausa.org

  Founded in 1980, the Brain Injury Association of America (BIAA) is the leading national organization serving and representing individuals, families and professionals who are touched by a life-altering, often devastating, traumatic brain injury.

- **The National Family Caregivers Association**
  www.thefamilycaregiver.org

  Offers extensive information on caregiving topics and member organizations.

- **The National Rehabilitation Information Center**
  www.naric.com

  A resource that touches on products and home modifications, this website gives results of federal research and lists other helpful programs and newsletters related to living with disabilities. There is a charge for some services.

- **The National Resource Center for Traumatic Brain Injury**
  www.neuro.pmr.vcu.edu

  The mission of the National Resource Center for Traumatic Brain Injury (NRCTBI) is to provide relevant, practical information for professionals, persons with brain injury, and family members. With more than two decades of experience investigating the special needs and problems of people with brain injury and their families, NRCTBI offers a wide variety of helpful materials for survivors and caregivers through its website and catalog.

Bibliography

American Heart Association. 2006. Accessed January 6, 2012. http://www.heart.org.

"Bob Woodruff." *ABC News.* October 14, 2008. Accessed October 25, 2011. http://abcnews.go.com/WNT/story?id=127761.

Brain Injury Peer Visitor Association. 2011. Accessed October 25, 2011. http://www.braininjurypeervisitor.org/.

Faul, Mark, Likang Zu, Marlena M. Wald, and Victor G. Coronado. *Traumatic Brain Injury in the United States: Emergency Department Visits, Hospitalizations, and Deaths.* Atlanta, GA: Centers for Disease Control and Prevention, National Center for Injury Prevention and Control, 2010. http://www.cdc.gov/traumaticbraininjury/pdf/blue_book.pdf.

Finkelstein, Eric, Phaedra Corso, and Ted Miller. *The Incidence and Economic Burden of Injuries in the United States .* New York: Oxford University Press, 2006.

"Gabby Giffords' Remarkable Recovery." *ABC News.* November 4, 2011. Accessed November 7, 2011. http://abcnews.go.com/WNT/video/gabby-giffords-remarkable-recovery-14885317.

"Glasgow Coma Scale." *Centers for Disease Control and Prevention.* May 9, 2003. Accessed January 6, 2012. http://www.bt.cdc.gov/masscasualties/pdf/glasgow-coma-scale.pdf.

Hagen, Chris, Danese Malkmus, and Patricia Durham. "Levels of Cognitive Functioning." *Rehabilitation of the Head Injured Adult: Comprehensive Physical Management*. Downey, CA: Professional Staff Association of Rancho Los Amigos National Rehabilitation Center, 1979.

Hanzman, Stuart. "Anger, Frustration and Anxiety: A Day in the Life of the Brain Injured." *Brain Injury Association of Georgia*. 2007. Accessed October 25, 2011. http://www.braininjurygeorgia. org/articles/anger_frustration_anxiety.pdf.

Johnson, Glen. *Traumatic Brain Injury Survival Guide*. June 25, 2010. Accessed October 25, 2011. http://www.tbiguide.com.

Kropa, Jean. "Care for the Caregiver." *Synergy HomeCare Newsletter*, April 2010. Accessed October 25, 2011. http://www.braininjurypeervisitor.org/index.php?p=1_35.

Kubler-Ross, Elisabeth. *On Death and Dying*. New York: Simon & Schuster/Touchstone, 1969.

Lemke, Denise M. "Riding Out the Storm: Sympathetic Storming after Traumatic Brain Injury." *The Journal of Neuroscience Nursing*, 36, no. 1 (2004): 4-9.

"Liam Neeson's wife, Natasha Richardson, Dies." *Belfast Telegraph*. March 19, 2009. Accessed Novermber 4, 2011. http://www. belfasttelegraph.co.uk/entertainment/film-tv/news/liam-neesons-wife-natasha-richardson-dies-14232651.html.

National Aphasia Association. 2009. Accessed October 25, 2011. http://www.aphasia.org.

Plitt, Todd. "Struggle for Words Frustrates Woodruff." *USA Today*. February 24, 2008. Accessed November 4, 2011. http://www.usatoday.com/news/health/2008-02-24-bob-woodruff_N.htm.

Regarding Henry. Directed by Mike Nichols. Hollywood, CA: Paramount Pictures, 1991.

Report to Congress on Mild Traumatic Brain Injury in the United States: Steps to Prevent a Serious Public Health Problem. Atlanta, GA: Centers for Disease Control and Prevention, National Center for Injury Prevention and Control, 2003. http://www.cdc.gov/ncipc/pubres/mtbi/mtbireport.pdf.

CPSIA information can be obtained at www.ICGtesting.com
Printed in the USA
LVOW041420170212

269052LV00002B/2/P